The Battle Lines of Worship

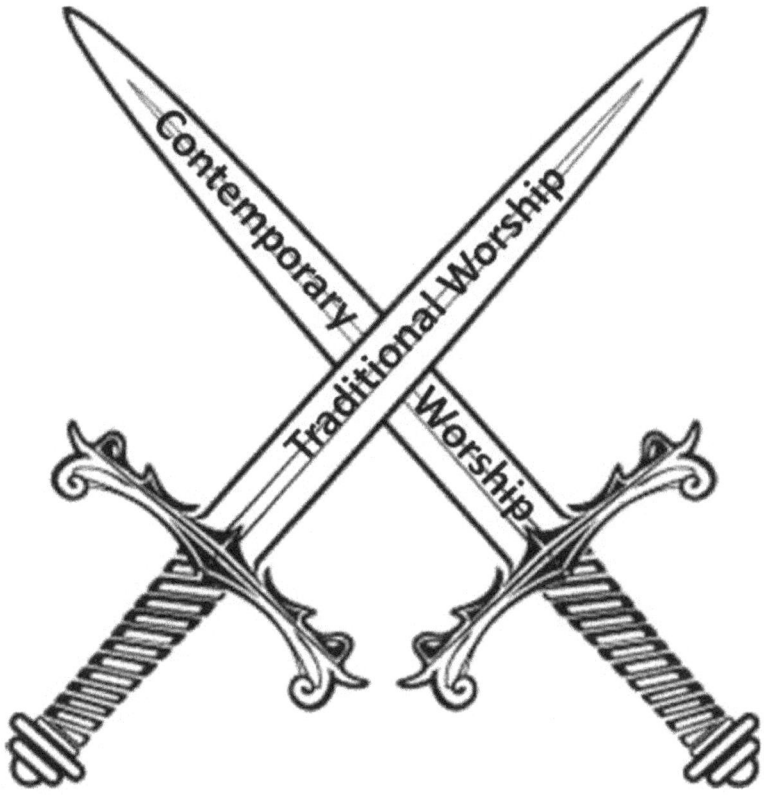

Contemporary Worship

Traditional Worship

Finding A Place Of Truce And Trust

Battle Lines of Worship
Finding a Place of Truce and Trust

Copyright ©2010 by D. Jonathan Watts

ISBN: 1-55605-406-8   978-1-55605-4068

Library of Congress Control Number: 2010935381

WYNDHAM HALL PRESS
5050 Kerr Rd
Lima, Ohio 45806
www.wyndhamhallpress.com

Printed in The United States of America

Battle Lines of Worship
Finding a Place of Truce and Trust

A Study To Explore The Tension
Between Worship Styles

D. Jonathan Watts, Ph.D.

Acknowledgments

As with any work there are more people involved with the process than the author.

The first person I would like to acknowledge is Mary Baker, a member of Guntersville First United Methodist Church and the Scruggs Sunday School Class. As I was about to begin the lesson of the day for the class Mary leaned over to me, and pointing to an underlined sentence in the Adult Sunday School book, said, "I can't wait until you talk about this!" "This" was a statement concerning proper worship. Intending to only address the statement briefly, the subject created a stirring debate which lasted for almost an hour. Mary Baker is the one who acted as the catalyst for this work.

I would also like to acknowledge my wife, Karen. As we walked together one morning I described for her my thoughts on writing an article on the tension between traditional and contemporary worship. Through her questioning and exploring the "article" became a book. Her patience and support throughout this effort of exploration and discovery has been invaluable.

Dr. Cynthia Denham and Mrs. Carolyn Bryson have worked tirelessly over this text. I have tried my best to listen to their expertise in gender, tense, and language as I held in tension the tales of the ancient past and the stories being created by this post-modern, digital Culture.

Table of Contents

Introduction

The lesson of the day in the large adult class was the familiar "fiery furnace" story. Why the author of the material had chosen this text to focus on worship was beyond me. I took my own approach to the story, which was to center on the faith of the three Hebrew boys. Just before I stepped to the lectern, a lady sitting next to me leaned over and whispered, "I can't wait until you get to this part!" "This part" was an underlined sentence concerning true worship.

I felt obligated to address the topic of worship before entering the Daniel story. After making a brief statement on my thoughts, I immediately found myself in the midst of a dark storm of thundering voices firing lightning bolts across the room and defending what they termed "right worship." They murmured about "those" who have taken "right worship" and watered it down, jazzed it up, and removed its spirituality. These people had grown the spiritual roots of their faith within the confines of what most term "traditional" worship. Not all were down on the contemporary style; a few came to the defense of friends and family. They were quick to add that if the contemporary style was what others liked, then let them have it.

As the class debated the issue, I was reminded of a similar situation a year prior. I had been asked to lead a retreat for those seeking a deeper spiritual journey. My task was to explore the topic of how a person senses the "call of God " on a one's life. During the weekend, the retreat leaders informed me the participants would have a dedicated block of time to ask questions. The session too quickly moved from "call" to worship to "right way" to worship. Again, I tried to explain the concept of how worship was to find oneself in the presence of God. Some find it in the silent moments of a service, while others find it in the singing of old hymns and ordered liturgy. Others find it in loud music, new choruses, and spontaneous change.

I did not get to the lesson I had prepared that Sunday morning. Rather, after an hour of debate and discussion, I felt more troubled than before. Why is it that we draw battle lines between the worship styles? Who has been granted the authority to use the term "right worship"? And why is this such a touchy subject on both sides of the fence? What could I do to help these people call a truce on the word war and find a place where they could not only understand the reason each group prefers a certain style of worship but also provide a place of trust—where each worship setting is given its proper respect by the others?

It would have been so wonderful if God had given us an instruction guide. Then we would know how long to hold people underwater at their baptisms, whether we use real wine when we celebrate the Lord's Supper, or if the appropriate time to worship is 11:00 a.m. on Sunday morning. But God did not provide us that information, so we must wade into the muddy water of tradition and doctrine. What follows is my attempt to address the issue of worship from a non-partisan approach, which allows each person to find where he or she attaches to the historical, traditional, and connective aspects of worship. And, as with every journey, I begin at the beginning—the real beginning.

Chapter 1

From the Beginning to a New Beginning
Concepts of Worship and Sacredness in Genesis
and Pre-Tabernacle Texts

When a person speaks of "worship" within the Judeo-Christian traditions, the word comes with preconceived concepts and established dogmas. If asked, most "church" people can define how "correct worship" should be experienced. We have accepted a belief that God began creation with a worship format already in place, and the way "we" worship God is the way humankind has always worshiped God. That is a misnomer. To gain a better perspective on the relationship of the Divine and humanity, we must begin at the beginning—before gold crosses, structured liturgy, and set-apart clergy to direct the pageant:

> *On the seventh day God finished the work that He had been doing, and He ceased (rested) on the seventh day from all the work that He had done. And God blessed the seventh day and declared it holy, because on it God ceased from all the work of creation that He had done.* (Genesis 2:2-3 JPS[i])

Notice God did not say the day would be holy because of worship but because it imitated the action of God. For generations upon generations, the "Sabbath" was set aside not for worship but for rest—to recreate. Many Jewish scholars believe the concept of the Sabbath as a day of study and worship did not occur until after the Babylonian Exile in 586 BC.

The first command of God to Adam was not to worship but to be a good gardener (Genesis 2:15). One can only speculate how long Adam and Eve were in the Garden before the fatal failure. Maybe they never had to stop and worship God—they walked with God during the "breezy time of the day" (Genesis 3:8 JPS).

The major shift came outside the garden and two sons later:

> *Abel became a keeper of sheep, and Cain became a tiller of the soil. In the course of time, Cain brought an offering to the Lord from the fruit of the soil; and Abel, for his part, brought the choicest of the firstlings of his flock. The Lord paid heed to Abel and his offering, but to Cain and his offering He paid no heed. Cain was much distressed and his face fell. (*Genesis 4:3-5 JPS)

It is impossible to count the number of pastors, preachers, and teachers who have painted the picture of these two brothers bringing their offerings to the LORD. We see them laying their gifts (Cain with his offering of fruit and Able the choicest from his flock) on a pile of rocks topped with wood and fire. Some have been guilty of creating an image of the event to formulate an explanation for why the LORD did not accept Cain's offering. Maybe the smoke from Cain's gift blew side-ways while Abel's ascended straight up. It has been said that Cain's offering was not accepted because it was not a "blood" sacrifice. That theory is dispelled later when the LORD instructs the people to bring both animal and crop sacrifices. The artistry of the storyteller helps us to recreate this scene in our imagination, thus helping us to gain a clearer image. Step by step one could create PowerPoint slides corresponding to the story. As the story is told verse by verse, a clearer image emerges. Surprisingly, one does not see a pile of rocks or a fire. And most of all, there is no sacrifice. We simply see two brothers bringing their gifts (an offering) and presenting them to the LORD. They may have had a special place to bring their gifts. Maybe they just found an appropriate spot to place the offerings and waited for the LORD to "receive" them. It could be that once placed before the LORD, God simply "beamed them up" as a sign of receiving and acceptance. We can speculate all day long, but in reality, anything we place in that void is only there by way of preconceived concepts or dreamed images.

What is strikingly absent from the text is a directive. We do not hear the LORD give directions or mandates on sacrifice and worship. Humanity seems to take the initiative as an act of gratitude and honor—not of requirement.

With a twist of the kaleidoscope, the image changes from the dying of one son and the casting out of the other to the birth of a third to Adam and Eve: *"Adam knew his wife again, and she bore a son and named him Seth, ... And to Seth, in turn, a son was born and he named him Enosh. It was then that **men began to invoke the LORD by name**"*(Genesis 4:25-26 JPS). Then humanity began to "worship" the LORD.

Noah was the first to offer a "burnt offering" to the LORD. After the flood event, the story continues,
> *So Noah came out, together with his sons, his wife, and his son's wives. Every animal, every creeping thing, and every bird, everything that stirs on earth came out of the ark by families.*
> *Then Noah built an altar to the Lord and, taking of every clean animal and of every clean bird, he offered burnt offerings on the altar. The Lord smelled the pleasing odor, and the Lord said to Himself: "Never again will I doom the earth because of man, since the devisings of man's mind are evil from his youth; nor will I ever again destroy every living being, as I have done."* (Genesis 8:18-21 JPS)

Built an altar!? Where did that idea come from? Noah

did not have any directive from the LORD demanding, commanding, or instructing humanity to build an altar. Neither do we find a word to humanity to burn a sacrifice—a concept which usually involves a live animal being slaughtered to show the LORD apprcciation or devotion. This first instance was no small thing. Notice the text identifies the "offering" to include specimens of all the animal kingdom, including every clean animal and every clean bird. What it does not say is whether all of these animals were sacrificed. This would have been a massive event—the slaughter of many animals. (Notice the word "sacrifice" is not used—we will find that word later). He had just been through the cleansing of the entire earth. Could it have been that he gathered all these "clean" creatures and offered an offering of aromatic plants that really did smell good? Burning hair and flesh cannot be described as "sweet smelling." Again, we can only speculate as to how this event played out. The ancient storytellers were not keen on particulars yet were very sharp on the outcomes.

What we do know is that the concept of building a holy icon was common among ancient peoples. We often term these sacred monuments totems, objects which symbolize to a community the sacredness of a particular place or event. The Native Americans of the North West created totem poles, which served as the story outline for their cultural history. Other cultures in India, Africa, and Europe had similar emblems of remembrance. When we look at the Egyptian pyramids or Stonehenge, even though we do not understand all the symbols and implications, we sense the spirit of sacredness. People in the current culture continue to build shrines as places of memory. Some can be found on the sides of many highways in the form of crosses and placards, often decorated on the anniversary of a fatal accident or the birthday of or a holiday missed by a loved one.

"Totems" described in the biblical text do not seem to

be objects of beauty. It appears the altars were built in haste and with materials at hand. What was handy? Rocks. I remember my dad relaying a conversation he had with a good friend who had just returned from a tour of the Holy Land. "Ralph," he said, "what did you see?" Ralph responded, "David, I saw rocks and rocks and more rocks." One might imagine how after an encounter with the Divine, the shaking hand grasps stones and shards and begins nervously stacking one upon the other as they created a memorial pillar—a symbol of a special event created out of a timeless element of stone. Piles of rocks became the sacred totems in the wilderness places.

What these totems do for a people is create an etiological check point. (Etiology is the study of causes— often referred to as the study of "why.") Especially in terms of the Hebrew people, a pile of rocks in an odd place raised the question "Why are these rocks here?" That opened the door for a teaching moment: "My child, our father Abraham met the Lord here one day and piled these stones as a remembrance."

Another word attached to many of these structures is "ebenezer." Every time I see or hear that word, two images cross my mind. The first is the character in Charles Dickens' A Christmas Carol—Ebenezer Scrooge, all gnarly and bent with an attitude to match. The other is a song "Come Thou Fount" written by a twenty-two-year-old Methodist pastor, Robert Robinson, in 1758.[2] Robinson's hymn is based on a text from 1 Samuel: *Samuel took a stone and set it up between Mizpah and Shen, and named it Ebenezer: "For up to now," he said, "the Lord has helped us"* (1 Samuel 7:12 JPS). As a child I was always drawn to the second verse—mostly because of the captivating imagery. The verse, as it appears in most hymnals, states: *Here I raise my Ebenezer / hither by Thy help I come. / And I hope, by Thy good pleasure, / safely to arrive at home.*

The word's root is Hebrew—*EbenEzer*, *Eben* (stone) and *Ezer* (place). The word is often defined as a place or stone of help, the "help" directed at drawing attention to the sacredness of that place upon which it stands.

The most prevalent places of totems are cemeteries, which display stones and monuments standing as remembrances. In ancient cemeteries are shards pressed into the ground with names and dates etched onto the faces of the stones. Later, the memorial stones became more ornate and were embellished with words from the deceased or a favorite Bible verse. Now, through modern technology, we can even see images of the person permanently engraved by laser in the headstone.

Totems and ebenezers are present in the sanctuaries of our churches as crosses, candles, Bibles, and fonts, representing and reminding us of something holy. In a spirit of reverence, we have come face-to-face with something holy—something we do not want to forget.

Interestingly, the earliest written record of the Great Flood is not found in the Hebrew text but in the Sumerian culture, which occupied the area later known as Babylon. Scholars tell us the earliest "written" form of the book of Genesis was penned around 900 BC. The Sumerian epic of the Great Flood was written on clay tablets, maybe as early as 3000 BC. The epic and the Genesis story tie the entire story together. Sumer inhabited the region also said to have been the site of the Garden of Eden. These clues lead to the region where Noah probably lived—where then, after the Great Flood, humanity settled and remained until they were spread abroad by the mysterious Tower of Babel event.

The next character in Genesis to appear was one first called Abram and later renamed Abraham. He comes from the line of Shem and begins his journey from the land of Ur, a city in the ancient Sumerian empire later known as Babylon or Mesopotamia. It was Abraham's father who began the journey leaving Ur and heading northward. Terah, Abraham's father, gathered Abraham and his wife Sarai (Sarah) along with Lot, his grandson, and moved from Ur to Haran. They stopped and "settled there" in a place later known as the "native" land of Abraham.

The reason why Abraham built altars and offered sacrifices seems to stem from his ancestry—the culture of Sumer known for its practices of both animal and human sacrifice.

The location of Sumer has its historical roots in the earlier story of the tower of Babel. When the people made the exodus from their "tower to God," those left behind became pagan. Sumer was a collection of twelve city/states, and each had its own specific god. Ur, the city of Terah and Abraham, worshiped the moon god Nanna (also known as Sin), who is portrayed on ancient tablets as an old man with a flowing beard. Much of the worship centered around fertility rites and celebrations, some of which were very explicit.

To the north, Haran, the sister city of Ur, worshiped the same god. Therefore, when Terah and his family moved north, they moved into a place where they found religious familiarity. So, this is where Abraham saw his example of worship and sacrifice. This is not advocating that our worship came from ancient Ur but rather that those early fathers and mothers worshiped in a way they understood, creating places of holiness and connection to the divine. Abraham did not build altars because of a command from God but because of his understanding of how one worships the Lord.

Somewhere along the way Abraham made a shift from

Nanna to YHWH, a tetragrammaton or letters, which
symbolize the name of God. An old rabbinical tale says Terah
was in the business of making idols. Abraham debated often
with his father about how these were only statues with no real
power, an argument often met with a father's firm scorn. One
day, while Terah was away, Abraham took a hammer and
crushed all the statues except the largest. He placed the
hammer in the hand of that statue. When his father came
home, he was livid at the destruction. "Who did this?" he
asked. Abraham first said, "The big god crushed the little
gods." Terah immediately scolded Abraham saying how that
could not be because the "god" was only a statue. It was on
that point Abraham made his case.

After receiving the call from the Lord to leave his
"native land"(which is now Haran), Abraham built several
altars/totems. Upon entering the land of Canaan, he paused at
Shechem. Abraham *"built an altar there to the LORD who had
appeared to him"* (Genesis 12: 7 JPS). After his journey into
Egypt, he returned to that altar and invoked the name of LORD
(Genesis 13:4), and at Mamre in Hebron he built an altar
(Genesis13:18).

The major shift comes in Genesis 15. The LORD again
told Abraham of future generations. This time, tired of
hearing all these promises, Abraham complained to the LORD
about being childless. The LORD commanded Abraham to get
a three-year-old heifer, a three-year-old she-goat, a three-year-
old ram, a turtledove, and a young bird. Abraham gathered
them and cut them into two pieces (except the young bird).
Then:

> *As the sun was about to set, a deep sleep fell upon*
> *Abram, and a great dark dread descended upon him.*
> *And [the LORD] said to Abram, "Know well that your*
> *offspring shall be strangers in a land not theirs, and*
> *they shall be enslaved and oppressed four hundred*

*years; but I will execute judgment on the nation they
shall serve, and in the end they shall go free with great
wealth. As for you, you shall go to your fathers in
peace; you shall be buried at a ripe old age. And they
shall return here in the fourth generation, for the
iniquity of the Amorites is not yet complete."
When the sun set and it was very dark, there appeared
a smoking oven, and a flaming torch which passed
between those pieces. On that day the Lord made a
covenant with Abram, saying, "To your offspring I
assign this land,"* (Gen 15:1218 JPS)

This was an unusual event of animals being slaughtered, but in
the bizarre vision the sacrifices were not burned or destroyed.
It seems as if they were left there for the birds of prey to
devour at a later time.

The first mention of sacrifice comes associated with
testing. We come to understand that sacrifice begins with the
destruction/death of something to "please" God.

*After these things God tested Abraham. He said
to him, "Abraham!" And he said, "Here I am." He
said, "Take your son, your only son Isaac, whom you
love, and go to the land of Moriah, and offer him there
as a burnt offering on one of the mountains that I shall
show you." So Abraham rose early in the morning,
saddled his donkey, and took two of his young men
with him, and his son Isaac; he cut the wood for the
burnt offering, and set out and went to the place in the
distance that God had shown him. On the third day
Abraham looked up and saw the place far away. Then
Abraham said to his young men, "Stay here with the
donkey; the boy and I will go over there; we will
worship, and then we will come back to you."
Abraham took the wood of the burnt offering and laid
it on his son Isaac, and he himself carried the fire and
the knife. So the two of them walked on together.*

Isaac said to his father Abraham, "Father!" And he said, "Here I am, my son." He said, "The fire and the wood are here, but where is the lamb for a burnt offering?" Abraham said, "God himself will provide the lamb for a burnt offering, my son." So the two of them walked on together. (Genesis 22:1-8 JPS)

In this story we experience the first use of the word "worship." In other passages where offerings were brought or an altar was constructed, they "invoked" the name of God. By definition these are two different events. "To invoke" means to call upon, to cry out to, or to summon. It creates the image of one looking heavenward and saying, "Hey! Are You paying attention?" To worship, rather, is to bring oneself into the presence of the Divine. It is more an act of humility and respect, and it puts a person on the receiving end.

As the history of a people unfold, we find only one incident where Isaac built an altar. That event took place at Beersheba after God appeared to him and renewed the Abrahamic covenant. There was no sacrifice, just the building of an altar and "invoking" the name of the LORD (Genesis 26:23ff).

This is in contrast to Jacob's experiences. We know the story of Jacob's dream of the ladder to heaven and God's promise to provide safety. There he took the stone he had used as a pillow, set it up as a pillar, and then poured oil on it as a sign of remembrance and sacredness. Jacob named the place Bethel. After his time of gaining two wives, two handmaidens, eleven sons and a daughter, he heard the call to go home. He wrestled the stranger and faced his brother in fear and trembling to find only open arms of acceptance. In Genesis 35, God speaks to Jacob saying,

> *" Arise, go up to Bethel and remain there; and build an altar there to the God who appeared to you*

*when you were fleeing from your brother Esau." So
Jacob said to his household and to all who were with
him, "Rid yourselves of the alien gods in your midst,
purify yourselves, and change your clothes. Come, let
us go up to Bethel, and I will build an altar there to the
God who answered me when I was in distress and who
has been with me wherever I have gone." They gave
to Jacob all the alien gods that they had, and the rings
that were in their ears, and Jacob buried them under
the terebinth that was near Shechem. ... Thus Jacob
came to Luz - that is, Bethel - in the land of Canaan,
he and all the people who were with him. There he
built an altar and named the site Elbethel, for it was
there that God had revealed Himself to him when he
was fleeing from his brother.* (Gen 35:17 JPS)

Here we find a new directive for approaching the
sacred totems. One was to cleanse themselves before
preparing the sacred place. This was once the standard for
attendance at a worship service—worshipers would put on
their "Sunday best" to go to church. In most cultures when
people meet for sacred events, they put on special clothes.
This is also an etiological event— it reminds people that this
is a sacred time, which calls for our best in everything—
spiritually and physically. This was recently voiced in an
article by Rachel Campos-Duffy:

> "Sunday best" has lost its meaning and fewer and
> fewer parents spend Saturday night scrubbing down
> kids in the bath and laying out clothes for the morning.
> The modern family is just too busy and "casual" for
> this kind of ritual. ...
> Dressing my kids for church is a nonverbal way of
> letting even our youngest child know that our church is
> an important place and Mass is an important event. ...
> The bottom line is that I go through the trouble out of
> respect for God and the other worshipers. ... At the

time and effort I put into bringing my family to His home freshly scrubbed, combed, and neatly dressed is part of my gift to Him. My God died on the cross for me. Dressing up to worship Him is the least I can do. [3]

Suddenly, we experience a void in the sacred spaces. Joseph never set up a pillar or burned an offering, and Moses, the chosen one, spent his nurturing years, not surrounded by the family stories of the Hebrews, but in the house of Pharaoh and the Egyptian culture. We understand that at some point Moses was told that he himself was not Egyptian but Hebrew, which was manifested in the killing of the Egyptian and his fleeing Egypt as a fugitive. It is not until the theophany, God's appearance on Mount Horeb, that we see Moses facing the Divine One in conversation and humility. Here he was told to take off his shoes because he was standing on holy ground. (This makes us wonder why we do not remove our shoes when we go into our places of worship.)

When Moses returned to Egypt, he did so with the request to let the people go to worship the "God of the Hebrews." We know the story takes the course of ten plagues before that request was granted. The people headed for the promised land but took a stop at Mount Horeb, where God began to turn a loose-knit menagerie of tribes into a holy nation. Moses was up on the mountain taking direct instructions from the LORD when the people below got impatient. Aaron, the brother of Moses, was asked to construct a god who could "go before" them since they suspected that Moses would never return. Aaron acted on that response and built a golden calf—an image which has its root in the Egyptian religions. At times we are too hard on a people literally wandering off from a place they called home for about 400 years and going to a place which is real only in their family stories. They saw the hand of God in the plagues, the parting of the sea, the leading of the people with fire and cloud, but now they do not see God or Moses. They need something to hold on to—to believe in—which is the form of a calf.

On the mountain, a people finally got direction and purpose. As God spelled out the constitution for a new nation, the "preamble" of sorts was in the form of a decalogue—ten words.

> *God spoke all these words, saying: I the LORD am your God who brought you out of the land of Egypt, the house of bondage: You shall have no other gods besides Me. You shall not make for yourself a sculptured image, or any likeness of what is in the heavens above, or on the earth below, or in the waters under the earth. You shall not bow down to them or serve them. For I the LORD your God am an impassioned God, visiting the guilt of the parents upon the children, upon the third and upon the fourth generations of those who reject Me, but showing kindness to the thousandth generation of those who love Me and keep My commandments. You shall not swear falsely by the name of the LORD your God; for the LORD will not clear one who swears falsely by His name. Remember the sabbath day and keep it holy. Six days you shall labor and do all your work, but the seventh day is a sabbath of the LORD your God: you shall not do any work - you, your son or daughter, your male or female slave, or your cattle, or the stranger who is within your settlements. For in six days the LORD made heaven and earth and sea, and all that is in them, and He rested on the seventh day; therefore the LORD blessed the sabbath day and hallowed it.* (Exodus 20:111 JPS)

In closing, these people called Hebrews and Israelites to this point, are not bound by religious practices, rituals, or ceremonies but by lineage and story. They have put sign-posts for all to see: a pile of rocks, the naming of a place, the ebenezer of remembrance. Whenever we find ourselves in the presence of the Divine, it creates a memory which will never be forgotten. This practice continues to this day as many persons experiencing a life-changing encounter can quickly relate the time and place of their connecting with the Divine.

These early patriarchs of the faith did not go to church or travel to a sacred place. Whenever and wherever they found themselves in the presence of God became the time and place to worship. They did not have to have a prescribed liturgy. All they needed to do was to pile up rocks. They may even have poured oil on a stone and given the place a name. They could offer up words or sacrifices to the Divine. Worship was not relegated to a time. Worship was spontaneous.

Questions For Reflection

1) When humanity was created , God did not expect man and woman to be subservient in acts of bowing down and worshiping. It appears God expected to build an intimate, relational companionship. How was this relationship manifested?

2) In the Cain and Abel story, Cain was distraught because God did not accept his offering. How do you feel when you do not think your gift is being accepted in the way that you wished?

3) Ancient people created for themselves a holy place or shrine where they experienced a special connection to God. Describe a special place you consider "holy."

4) Abraham heard the voice of God calling him to leave his native land and simply follow God's lead. If you heard the voice of God calling you to do something which involved risk, how would you respond?

5) Respond to the statement concerning the essence of this chapter: Worship was not relegated to a time but was intended to be spontaneous.

Endnotes

[1]

Tanakh: The Holy Scriptures : A New Translation of the Holy Scriptures According to the Traditional Hebrew Text. Philadelphia : Jewish Publication Society, 1997.

[2] Robert Robinson, "Come Thou Fount." Wyeth's Repository of Sacred Music, Part Second, 1813.

[3] Rachel Campos-Duffy, "Have We Become Too Casual? Why I Dress My Kids Up for Church." http://www.parentdish.com/2010/06/09/have-we-become-too-casual-why-i-dress-my-kids-up-for-church/.

Chapter 2

A Wandering House for a Wandering People
"Not all who wander are lost."—J.R.R. Tolkien

The worship journey now faced a major paradigm shift. Once Moses descended from the mountain, with commandments in his hand and laws on his lips, a triad of dramatic shifts occurred for the people. The first obvious triad began in exile. The family clan, known as Hebrews to the outside and Israelites to members of the families, grew from a group of seventy (those numbered as entering Egypt) into a multitude. After four hundred years, the "aliens" were led out of Egypt to a land they called their own. They were no longer a single family group but rather a nation of twelve strongly independent tribes/clans.

The second part of the triad is the Israelites' move from a people of spontaneity to a people of structure and law. Before the exodus, the Hebrew/Israelite people basically lived a faith of instinct and emotion. They worshiped, sacrificed, and prayed in times of need, celebration, and conflict. A later book says "*all the people did what was right in their own eyes*" (Judges 21:25 NRSV). Now there are rules, lists, dos and don'ts. This change opens the door for someone to lift the accusing finger announcing, "Hey! You can't do that."

The third and final shift, and probably the most powerful, is the move from a people who met God in the wilderness to a people who now house God in a particular space. Before this change the people met God in dreams, on stony ground, and out in the dusty places (as the name Hebrew often translates—"the dusty ones"). They are now moving into a culture which points to a specific place, declaring "God is here!"

To expand upon the paradigm shifts, until the exodus event these people worshiped a God who met them on the road, on the mountain, and in the dark. They placed etiological markers as signposts and places of remembrance. A pile of stones reminded them of a heavenly encounter. A city was given a name because of a holy experience. They kept the faith alive by telling the stories as they lay under canopies of stars, gazing into the vast unknown, to relive the experiences of a God whose name they did not even know.

The small bands of wanderers have grown into a mighty force as Genesis 46 recalls,

> *All the persons belonging to Jacob who came to Egypt - his own issue, aside from the wives of Jacob's sons - all these persons numbered sixty-six. And Joseph's sons who were born to him in Egypt were two in number. Thus the total of Jacob's household who came to Egypt was seventy persons.* (Genesis 46:27 JPS)

Four hundred years of growth, prosperity, and slavery stand as a great chasm between the time of Joseph and the leadership of Moses. Now, as they moved towards the Promised Land, the men (twenty years and older who could serve as a military force) numbered 603,550 excluding the Levites per the instruction of God (Numbers 2:32).

God called Moses to the top of the mountain to receive the constitution of a new nation. We like to "see" Moses coming down from the mountain with the tablets in hand ready to say, "I got the rules; now let's go!" The accounts in Exodus, Deuteronomy, Numbers, and Leviticus make us realize these events, in reality, are only the tip of the iceberg. After hearing the volumes of rules and directions, we wonder how Moses could keep it all straight. It could be that here is where his upbringing in the palace of Pharaoh came in handy.

I suspect, as an educated person, he knew how to read and write. Maybe Moses did indeed bring, rolled up in his back pocket, the constitution for a new nation dictated by God and scribed by Moses himself. Yet this single experience removed the freedom of intuition and tugged one's spirit to shift into the legalistic culture ready to point to a line in a text declaring, "See, it says so right here!" Of course, it is understood that these ancient storytellers had remarkable recall, and Moses may have orated these rules and regulations to the other storytellers who absorbed these words into their very beings.

As they prepared to move toward a new home, Moses had been instructed to create a special place of worship, which was both symbolic and mobile. The Tabernacle was to be placed in the center of the community. This was not to be a permanent, stationary place but a movable sanctuary. This space to be God's house was a tent in the midst of a people who dwelled in tents. All the materials used in the building of the Tabernacle were to be gifts freely given by the people. In Exodus 25 the voice of the LORD dictated to Moses instructions for building the Tabernacle and the inauguration of a Priesthood.

The best way for us to experience this place is simply to take a walk. Our journey begins in the midst of the people. The Tabernacle is in the center of the camp surrounded by the segregated clans of the Israelites. Each tribe has its prescribed location in relationship with the Tabernacle. The first thing we see on this journey is a wall created by poles and curtains. The footprint of the Tabernacle is only 150 feet long and 75 feet wide. This is unusually small, considering it is enveloped by up to a million people (by some estimates, which includes all—women, children, and the elderly) and their tents.

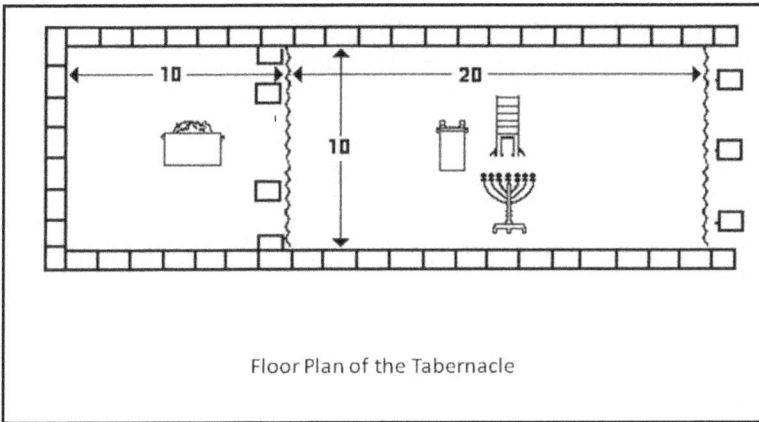

Floor Plan of the Tabernacle

Approaching the Tabernacle, we begins by circumventing a 7.5 foot wall made of linen curtain, broken on the east side by a three-panel section woven of blue, purple, and scarlet. This is the entrance into the sacred space. The material is defined as "fine twisted linen" — hardly the image of the kind of cloth for those who were brick masons and shepherds. On many occasions a person would glance backward over a shoulder to catch a glimpse of Egypt. This includes remembering not only the experience but also the lessons learned. The art of weaving this cloth may have been perfected while they lived as aliens in Egypt.

Entering the courtyard, we immediately encounter the Altar, a bronze box 7.5 feet square and 4.5 feet high. It is a free-standing place of sacrifice, which can be transported by poles inserted through rings mounted on each side. This is the place of sacrifice where the people of God come to offer gifts, to seek forgiveness, to make atonement, or to give thanks. These sacrifices are not particularly corporate but serve as a place for the individual to connect with the Divine. The odor of the burning sacrifices rises upward to carry the prayers up to God and the sins into the realm of "forgotten." Nothing indicates this is anything other than a place for the men to present themselves before God. Since the society is strongly patriarchal, the women and children stay home.

Just beyond the Altar is a large washing basin called the Laver. This is the first indication that as we move deeper into the space, we are also moving into a more sacred space. The Laver was to be used by the priests ritually to wash their hands and feet before coming into the presence of the Holy, much like saying the blessing before the meal. This also serves as a line of demarcation separating the ordinary people from those set apart. Only the priest could enter the next area of the Tabernacle called the Tent of Meeting - the "Royal Residence" of God.

The visual cues make us aware that the closer we come to the Holy, the more costly the materials used. Outside in the courtyard the appointments are bronze. Inside the Tent of Meeting the metal is gold.

The "Tent,"15 feet wide and 45 feet long, is divided into two sacred spaces. The Holy Place can be entered only by the priests. The Holy of Holies can be entered only by the High Priest and then only once a year. We often think of this space as a tent, but it is better described as a walled enclosure with a tarp-type top or covering. The materials used to create this sacred space are gold; silver; copper; blue, purple, and crimson yarns; fine linen; goat's hair; and various treated hides.

The wall structure is acacia wood, per the instruction of the LORD. This light, hard, and durable wood turns ebony black with age. The wall of wood is overlaid with pure gold. Gold is not only an element of value but also serves, in this setting, as a reflecting agent.

Entering this space, we proceed through curtains,

which speak of richness and elegance. Only the finest materials are used, even woven gold. The Holy Place, or the first room in the Tent of Meeting, is 15 feet wide and 30 feet long. On the left side of the room is a golden lamp stand called a Menorah, shaped similarly to a tree with six branches (three on each side), the trunk extending past the limbs. A lamp tops each of the seven branches and provides light for the room by reflecting off the golden walls. Imagine stepping into a room with polished, pure gold walls.

Across the room, to the right, is the Table of Shewbread. On this table the priests would place twelve loaves of bread, representing the twelve tribes of Israel. The loaves were replaced each week by fresh bread. This table also held the offerings of the First Fruits.

At the center of the room, near the rear is the Altar of Incense. The rising smoke and sweet fragrance carried the prayers of the people heavenward. Also called the Golden Altar, this square box is similar to the altar in the courtyard but on a much smaller scale.

Finally, we steal a glimpse inside the most sacred of spaces, the Holy of Holies. Reflecting off the gold walls inside this space is only one appointment — the Ark of the Covenant, also known as the Ark of the Pact. In Exodus 25:10ff we read:

> *Tell the people to build a chest of acacia wood forty-five inches long, twenty-seven inches wide, and twenty-seven inches high. Cover it inside and out with pure gold and put a gold edging around the lid. Make four gold rings and fasten one of them to each of the four legs of the chest. Make two poles of acacia wood. Cover them with gold and put them through the rings, so the chest can be carried by the poles. Don't ever remove the poles from the rings. When I give you the*

*Ten Commandments written on two flat stones, put
them inside the chest.*

*Cover the lid of the chest with pure gold. Then
hammer out two winged creatures of pure gold and
fasten them to the lid at the ends of the chest. The
creatures must face each other with their wings spread
over the chest. Inside it place the two flat stones with
the Ten Commandments and put the gold lid on top of
the chest. I will meet you there between the two
creatures and tell you what my people must do and
what they must not do. The LORD said: No lampstand
or lights are in this space. God's presence provides the
light.* (Exodus 25:10ff CEV[1])

This wooden box is covered inside and out with gold.
The top, with its two Cherubs, is solid gold. Inside are three
very important items: a jar of manna, the budding rod of
Aaron, and the two tablets of commandments carved by the
finger of God.

This most sacred of space, which has no windows, is
illuminated only by the very presence of God. Leaving this
place as we finish our journey, we are suddenly aware that
everything constructed for the Tabernacle was designed to be
carried. This indeed was a mobile house.

The second unit of the worship establishment focused
on a new order of selected or ordained clergy—set apart to do
the work of worship. Until this time, it was the responsibility
of the families to pass on the stories of the founding fathers.
Worship, as we presume it (gathering, singing, praising,
prayers, exhortation, etc.), did not exist. Worshipers could
talk about YHWH God, but there were no Bibles, icons, or
liturgy to tell them HOW to worship. Now there are rules,
expectations, ritual, a place to perform cultic rites along with
selected leadership to help those along on the spiritual path.

The tribe singled out for a holy purpose is Levi. They seem to have come into special favor when they aided Moses in the quelling of the Golden Calf event. This tribe, prior to this point, had no special spiritual gifts. They were, for lack of a better term, as secular as the other tribes. Now they faced a major vocational shift from shepherds of sheep to shepherds of God's flock.

One way God separated this new order was by a visible clue—the way they dressed. It was understood that the clothes made the priest. Once the individuals had finished their religious duty and removed the Priestly Garments, they became ordinary men. They were not to perform any religious tasks unless they put on the priestly garments. The "ordinary" priest wore four worship garments: linen undergarments, a linen tunic, a linen belt or sash, and a turban. These garments were never to be washed. Once they became soiled, they were discarded in a way so no one could use the material, and new vestments were made. I assume these garments would have to be in ready supply since the priests were constantly sacrificing animals and burning offerings of different types.

There was no provision for shoes. They did the work of God barefoot—a visible remembrance of the Theophany event when Moses met God at the burning bush. It was on the side of Mount Horab that Moses turned aside to see a blazing bush. As he approached, he was instructed to remove his shoes because he was standing on holy ground. Where the priests served is now holy and sacred space.

High Priest, Priest, and Levite (Public Domain Image)

The vestments of the High Priest were much more elaborate. The instructions from God lists seven garments (eight if one includes the underpants made of linen). An ankle-length linen tunic with long sleeves, served as the inner garment. The outer robe, called an Ephod, was slightly shorter with shorter sleeves. This robe was blue, God's color, according to the Jewish community since sky and water are blue. The Ephod, or apron, was embroidered with blue, purple, scarlet, and gold threads. On the hem were embellishments of dyed wool in the shape of pomegranates. Also attached to the hem were golden bells. Their exact purpose is unknown. One explanation is that they prevented the priest from "sneaking up on" God. In the later temple, they seemed to be used by the one responsible for keeping the lamps trimmed and burning in the Holy of Holies. As long as the bells were ringing, the priest was carrying out his duty. If the bells stopped ringing, there was cause for concern.

Over the top of the Ephod hung the Breastplate, a symbolic plate containing twelve precious stones (four rows of three) representing the twelve tribes. The shoulder straps had onyx plates on which the name of each tribe was inscribed—six on each shoulder. The little known element of this vestment was a small pocket which held the Urim and Thummim, two instruments of decision. Often thought to be sticks, dice, pebbles or even gem stones, some had described them as having the designated colors of black and white. In essence, the purpose of these was the casting of lots for understanding Divine direction. If a person came to the priest with a question, perhaps "Should I buy this land?" or "Is this the one I should marry?" and there was no clear direction on an answer, the priest would pull out the Urim and Thummim and, for lack of a better understanding, cast the lots. These instruments offered three possibilities: yes, no, and wait. Some say these two objects represented revelation and truth; others say these were divine names which could not be erased. That is, once the "stones" have spoken, the answer is fixed. The Ephod was kept in place by a Girdle, a shash woven with the same fabrics and pattern as the Ephod.

The final vestment was a two-part turban or hat. The turban was made of linen fabric wrapped around the head. Surrounding the base of the High Priest's turban was a golden band or plate on which was inscribed "Holy Unto the LORD." The turban was held in place by blue ribbons.

Israel now had a worship space and persons to lead worship, but how *did* they worship? It is quite evident they did not gather on the Sabbath day as a collective people to sing, pray, and listen to a proclamation. Daily sacrifices were carried out for the community or by individuals for the sake of forgiveness, praise, or homage to the LORD. No "sabbath" worship was carried out since that day, the seventh day, was not a day of worship but a day of rest. The people worshiped during the other six days. With such a small space available to the public, the outer courtyard of the Tabernacle would not accommodate even a single tribe inside the tabernacle complex at one time.

The task of the priests was not as "preacher" but as servant. The priests did the work of the LORD on behalf of all the people. There was no shortage of priests since these designated servants were all the men of the Tribe of Levi. They carried out their visible duties around the Altar and in the courtyard for all to see, but only the priests were allowed inside the holy tent where God's presence was experienced.

This mobile "house of God" was constructed for a short sojourn to the Promised Land. That idea was quickly abandonded upon the report of the twelve spies and, thus, the refusal of the people to move forward into the land. The Tabernacle wandered with the people for forty years. It is assumed that the Tabernacle crossed the Jordan River under the leadership of Joshua, but there is no specific mention of the holy place traversing the river. The only item noted at the crossing is the Ark of the Covenant. Joshua 3 describes the crossing of the Jordan and how Joshua instructed the priest to lead the processional with the Ark. Suddenly the object hidden from view deep inside the Holy of Holies is not only visible but on exhibit before the people.

The tabernacle wandered in the new land until it came to rest in Shiloh: *"Then the whole congregation of the Israelites assembled at Shiloh, and set up the tent of meeting there. The land lay subdued before them"* (Joshua 18:1 JPS). In its history at Shiloh, the Mishnah records that the wooden walls were replaced by stone walls but the covering (the roof of animal hide) remained. References to the Tabernacle and the Ark are many and can be studied through other resources, but we do understand it survived 369 years. Here the scriptures tell how the priests forgot the sacredness of their calling and did evil things, which brought expulsion of some priests from service.

Concluding this section, I make three particular observations. One, by intention, the place of worship, the Tabernacle, stood at the center of the community. It began in the midst of the community as they camped around the Holy Place. Then it was at Shiloh, a central place in the newly conquered land. Was it God's intention that the place of worship stand at the heart of community? We do not have to be historical scholars to realize there has been a major shift from that central place. Or has it? Could it be that worship is no longer the "center of community" but now focuses on the central core of an individual? That was, in fact, the way these people worshiped. The "place" stood in the center, but the "act of worship" was primarily individual.

Second, those who led worship were intentionally separated from the laity. They were separated by the work they did—and only they could do it. They were also separated by the garments they wore—not everyday clothing but sacred clothing. I often hear pastors justify leading worship in jeans and t-shirts (or even a coat and tie) by claiming that they are "trying to be like the people." God never intended the one leading worship to be just another person. The leaders were to be called out, separated, holy persons doing a sacred task. This stigma is still evident today. I often tell of the time I went to a football game where all those around me were yelling at the top of their lungs the harsh criticisms aimed at the officials or other team. All went well until someone walked by and yelled at me, "Hello, Preacher!" From that moment on, those around me took a more subdued approach to the game. It was not me but the office I held that made the difference. Those called by God to lead the people, whether they want to embrace it or not, are set apart—by God and by those they serve.

Finally, even though there was a "worship place," at this point in history there was no sense of corporate worship.

Sure, there were special observances by the entire nation, but the most holy of all nights, the evening of the Passover Seder, was celebrated at home with family. So, worship began as a personal initiative to move toward God and not as a corporate gathering. To come to church for any other reason than to worship God is not worship.

Questions for Reflection

1) God instructed Moses to construct a Tabernacle to house God's presence. What is your response to the law stating that the Tabernacle was to be entered only by men and not the entire community?

2) In the instructions God provided for worship, the tribe of Levi held the responsibility to be priest to the people. They were priests because they were born into a family lineage of priests. How are the religious leaders in your faith community selected?

3) The High Priest had the Umin and Thummin to help him make decisions when neither he or the one bringing the question could discern the right choice. How do we, in a post-modern society discern God's will when we cannot seem to find a clear direction?

4) The priest wore special garments (vestments) while performing the service in God's Tabernacle. In your opinion, should those who lead worship today wear special garments which set them apart from the congregation? Did this directive apply only to the Jewish community?

5) In the age of the Tabernacle there was no designated time for the entire community to gather for worship and to receive instruction. Each person came as they felt led or sensed the need. What draws us to the place of worship?

Endnotes

[1] Contemporary English Version. New York: American Bible Society, 1995.

Chapter 3

The House Where God Lives
Worship Practices in the Temple
and the Synagogue

At the door of the tabernacle at Shiloh one thing was evident—the religious purity of the Levites did not remain intact. The early chapters of I Samuel tell the story of the boy Samuel. At a young age Samuel was visited by the Lord and told to issue a decree to the sons of Eli, who were doing what was evil in the sight of the Lord. This was the first of many prophetic cries for the wayward children to return to a higher standard.

During this time many Israelites made an annual pilgrimage to Shiloh to present their offerings to God. Yet, as a scattered and disjointed people, they constructed many "altars" where people would gather, offer a sacrifice, and pray in the interim. At Beth-el, Gibeon, and Shiloh, daily services of sacrifice were conducted. During this phase of Israel's history, sacrifice equaled worship.

The first critical move came when David, King of Israel, decided the presence of God should dwell in the capital city of Jerusalem. It made sense. Here is where Abraham met Melchizedek, King of Salem and priest of the Most High God. Tradition speaks of this mount as being the place where Abraham later took Isaac, as commanded by God, to be sacrificed. Tradition puts Jacob in this place when he had his angelic vision of the stairway to heaven. Salem, now Jerusalem, was the epicenter of a growing and prosperous nation.

After two attempts David finally brought the Ark to Jerusalem. It arrived as a symbol of God's presence among the people. David set it up in a tent (where the future Temple would be built) and the priests sacrificed burnt offerings (I Chronicles 16). One mystery was the question: What was inside the ark? Did it still contain the manna, Aaron's rod, and the tablets of the commandments? Since the Ark had been in the possession of the Philistines for about seven months, did they dare open the sacred box? And if they did, did they have the same experience as those in the Indiana Jones movie with the rushing around of destructive forces? It was not that dramatic. According to I Samuel, the stealing of the Ark brought severe hemorrhoids upon the Philistines so they decided to sent it back to the Israelites. 2 Chronicles states: *There was nothing inside the Ark but the two tablets that Moses placed there at Horeb, when the Lord made a Covenant with the Israelites after their departure from Egypt.* (2 Chronicles 5:10 JPS)

David settled into his comfortable palace, yet he struggled with the issue that he was living in luxury and the Ark of the Covenant (the presence of God) was dwelling in a tent. The prophet Nathan was commissioned by God to give David the bad news that he would not be allowed to build a permanent place for the Ark. That task would be reserved for his son. In 1 Kings 1 David selected Solomon as heir to the throne. Solomon was not his oldest son but the son of his favorite wife Bathsheba.

Once Solomon blueprinted the new Temple, it seemed counter-cultural that the Temple was not build with volunteer labor as was the Tabernacle. It was constructed with forced labor. The workforce is listed in 1 Kings 5.
    Solomon ordered thirty thousand people from
    all over Israel to cut logs for the temple, and he put
    Adoniram in charge of these workers. Solomon

*divided them into three groups of ten thousand. Each
group worked one month in Lebanon and had two
months off at home.*

*He also had eighty thousand workers to cut
stone in the hill country of Israel, seventy thousand
workers to carry the stones, and over three thousand
assistants to keep track of the work and to supervise
the workers. He ordered the workers to cut and shape
large blocks of good stone for the foundation of the
temple.* (1 Kings 5:13 - 17 CEV)[1]

It took seven years to construct the Temple and thirteen years
to complete Solomon's palace.

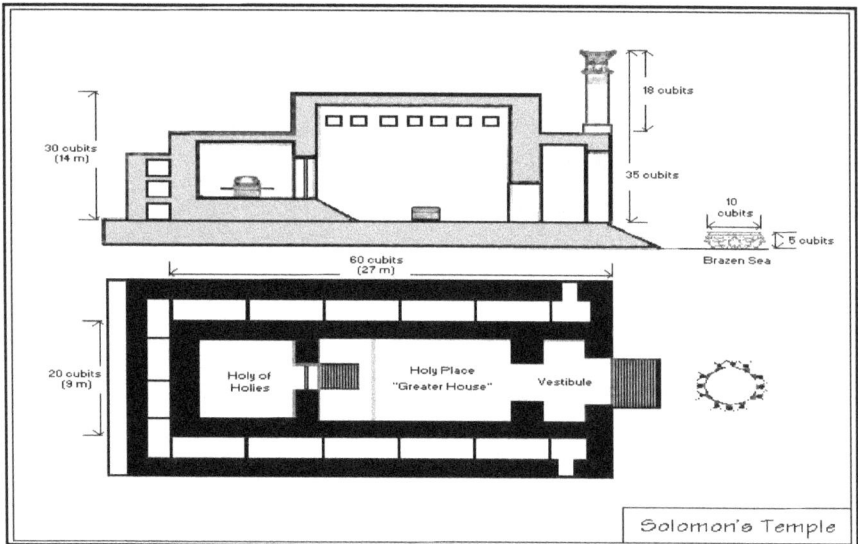

Solomon's Temple (Public Domain Image)

For all practical purposes, Solomon's Temple doubled
the size of the Tabernacle. The exact details and
measurements of the entire Temple complex are not recorded.
The entrance to a newly created Great Court via a stairway of
seven steps was the first indication this place was to be a holy
place not only set apart but also elevated to signify sacredness.

Some say the courtyard was an outer boundary which did not extend far beyond the next courtyard. Others say it was a large courtyard housing both the Temple and the Palace.

Entry into the sacred space was a gate which, as did the curtains of the Tabernacle, separated the outside world from the holy. This Upper Court or Inner Court, if the model to "double the size" was correct, could be as large as 100 feet wide and 300 feet long. For a visual reference, the courtyard was as long as a football field and almost as wide. A thick wall created the perimeter of the complex. Stepping into the courtyard, one came immediately come face-to-face with the large elevated bronze altar. To the left was a bronze vessel called the Molten Sea, which held the water for purification of the priest. This was an enormous vessel holding between 10,000 to 12,000 gallons of water. Ten other small lavers were placed on carts with wheels. These held water for sacrificial purification.

One imagines a temple as an image of tall spires and ornate contours surface. This structure was much like a box— a tall box surrounded by lower boxes. The tall core, the Temple, surrounded by shorter store-rooms, was 90 feet long, 30 feet wide, and 45 feet high. The Temple building contained the Holy of Holies and Holy Place. It was constructed as a pre-fabricated building. The stones were cut to size off-site at the quarry and then assembled on-site. People entered the space by ascending a set of steps to a porch 30 feet wide and 15 feet deep. Two massive bronze columns, stood outside the door to the Temple. These ebenezers, named Boaz (He is strong) and Jachin (He makes secure), were symbols of remembrance.

The first room was the Holy Place, which was 60 feet long, 30 feet wide, and 30 feet high with small windows around the top. Here the appointments of the Tabernacle were expanded. There were ten lamp stands and ten tables for Showbread. Near the back and center was the Altar of Incense. The walls were first covered with cedar boards. The ceiling was flat with beams and boards of cedar. The floor was overlaid with pine. All of the inner surfaces, covered with gold, were decorated with images of palm trees, flowers and winged cherubim.   Even the floor was covered with gold.

This Great Hall was decorated with carvings and flowers (calyxes). A set of steps rose to a space that formed a perfect cube 30 feet wide, 30 feet long, and 30 feet wide. Inside this room were only four objects. Two were massive cherubim, celestial creatures considered guardians, having the wings of an eagle, the head of a human, and the body of a lion. Each cherubim had a wingspan of fifteen feet so the wings touched the walls and each other.

The third object was the "foundation stone," located between the wings of the cherubim. A rabbinical legend says when Kind David began preparing the foundation of the capital city, a stone was found with the holy name of God etched into it. This was thought to be the stone where Jacob rested his head the night he had the vision of the angels going up and down the ladder to heaven. Jacob declared this place the "gateway to heaven." This stone became the "foundation stone."

With the cherubim facing the entrance with their wings outstretched, the fourth object was the Ark of the Covenant. By some counts there were only three objects. Wherever that list appears, the missing object is the foundation stone.

The interior of the Temple was decorated with carvings and everything was covered completely with "pure gold." Again, as with the Tabernacle, the common person would never be allowed to see the interior of the Temple—only the priests had that privilege. The Holy of Holies stood as the highest place in the Temple complex. At the Tabernacle, the further a person moved into the center towards the Holy Place, the more sacred the space. In the Tabernacle, to be near the Holy, it was how deep one went into the space. In the Temple it was how high one went which brought one closer to the Holy. The higher the people go, in their minds and hearts, the closer they get to God.

Worship continued to be primarily a sacrificial event. There were grand gatherings during the major festivals: the spring festivals of Passover and Pentecost, and the fall festival of the Booths or Tabernacles. Times of personal celebration or penitence, the purpose of the events was to present an offering to the Lord. There were times of collective celebration but, in the truest sense, not a time for collective worship. Evidence reveals there was an added element of chanting and prayers, which allowed the common person to connect to the sacrificial moment, and between the sound and the sacrifice stood the priests. As a priest offered up the sacrifices, other priests would raise their hands and offer a blessing and a benediction. Along with the chants and prayers developed the introduction of instrumental music. During the burning of the sacrifices, the Levites would sing, often accompanied by instruments. According to some scholars, a number of psalms, including some Davidic psalms, were chanted and sung with accompaniment.

After the death of Solomon, greed and pride caused the shattering of the united kingdom. Rehoboam, son of Solomon, rose up in great arrogance. This caused a great rift among the tribes, and the kingdom divided. Israel, comprised of ten tribes, formed the northern kingdom. The tribes of Judah and Benjamin formed the southern kingdom of Judah. The northern kingdom struggled with the realization that it did not have access to the Temple. Eventually the people created golden bulls, a representation of the golden calf in the wilderness, and declared these were the gods that brought them out of Egypt. In 721 B.C. the northern kingdom was conquered and disappeared.

The southern kingdom, Judah, had its ups and downs. It too fell to the forces of Nebuchadnezzar in 586 B.C. Not only were a large number of people carried into Babylonian exile, but also the Temple was robbed of its riches, stripped of its wealth, and completely destroyed. It was in this foreign land the people struggled with their distance from the "promised" land. They questioned if God would forget them and let them die, lost and alone as exiles. One of the major theological awakenings happened during the Babylonian exile—a realization that the God of Abraham, Isaac, and Jacob would not leave them alone and was able to be in their midst even as aliens.

During this period the people sought a "word" from God. They gathered around the prophets and listened to them. God did not have a house, but the prophets gave God a voice for the people. They would listen to the proclamation, ask questions for direction, and, in a communal sense, pray for each other and to God.

Another crisis arose while exiled in Babylon. The people began to fear that those back home and those away from home would forget the stories which bound together this fragmented flock. So, upon their return, three things occurred. First, they rebuilt a place of worship in Jerusalem. Second, they decided to systematically gather the stories of the people and write them down for future generations. And third, they created spaces to gather as communities to tell the stories, pray, and worship.

Upon the return from exile, Nehemiah led the people

in restoration. The Second Temple, built by Nehemiah, was much more modest than the First Temple. All the Temple vessels had been stolen; all that was left was the foundation. Historians note the footprint of the first structure was that of the second structure which reverted to a Tabernacle model with only one golden lamp stand and one table of Showbread in the Holy Place. Most striking of all, there were no doors. Both the entrance onto the Holy Place and the Holy of Holies were draped with heavy curtains, and nothing separated the Holy Place from the Holy of Holies except one object. The Ark was gone. The cherubim absent. The only thing in the Holy of Holies was the "foundation stone" on which the Ark once rested. The rock was considered the center or navel of the world. Here at the center the people could connect to God.

The worship experience itself went through changes. Now collections of psalms, prayers, and benedictions were proclaimed regularly. A. Z. Idelsohn writes:

> The service of the Temple is retained in the *Mishna* Tamid V. According to Rabbinical interpretation of that report, the priest would recite every morning the benediction *Ahava*, the Decalogue, the paragraphs of *Sh'ma*, the *Geula*, then the third benediction of Sh'ma, ... and the Priestly benediction.[2]

There were additional prayers and recitations on the Sabbath and holy days. Temple worship continued to be a sacrificial event. As sacrifices were made, the priest would recite or chant psalms or songs as those who brought the sacrifice would pray.

At this same time, local places of worship, called Synagogues, arose. These were not to replace the importance of the Temple but were to provide a place of constant connection to the people's history and destiny. The people could learn and experience at the Synagogue, but they could receive atonement only at the Temple.

After the exile to Babylon, the people feared that if that type of event ever happened again, the bonding stories of a people would be forgotten. So, the Synagogue system was established in almost every Jewish community. The Synagogue as a building was designed to be a multi-purpose building, more like a town hall. It was a gathering place for all types of events and meetings. The Sabbath took on new meaning. It changed from a day of rest to a day of worship.

Now the people had a place to gather as a community. The common name for this place was "beit tefilah," a house of prayer. It evolved as a place not only of prayer but also of instructions and education. Many synagogues housed sacred libraries.

As the community of faith continued to evolve, there arose a pattern of worship which gave direction and purpose to the gathering. Benjamin Williams and Harold Anstall describe the pattern of worship as follows:

1. The Litany. The first and opening part of the synagogue service was a series of prayers, a litany, blessing God for His love toward mankind. In its present form, the Orthodox liturgy begins with the Great Litany. The celebrant says, "In peace let us pray to the Lord," and the people respond, as they do to each of the following petitions, "Lord, have mercy."
2. The Confession. The Litany was immediately followed by a confession of God's faithfulness and of mankind's sin. In the Orthodox Liturgy, these may be found in the prayer between the Great Litany and the Scripture reading.
3. Intercessory Prayer. The third part was the Eulogy, the prayers of intercession. Likewise, these intercessory prayers complement the confessions in preparation for the Scripture readings.
4. Scripture Readings. This was followed by the

Reading from the Law and the Prophets. In today's Orthodox Church, as with any church using lexionary readings, these include Old Testament readings as well as Epistle and Gospel readings.

5. Preaching. The reading was followed by a discourse or sermon which expanded upon the reading and clarified its application to daily life. This is the homily or sermon in modern services.

6. Benediction. The service concluded with a Benediction, which means "good word."[3]

Here is the basis of "worship." Temple worship continues to be sacrificial. People journeyed to the Temple to offer sacrifice. There were no Sabbath services and no formal gatherings for song and prayer outside the holy days. The Temple was build as a fitting place for the Ark of the Covenant. The Temple was not a place to worship—it was God's house. This was where God lived. This was where God was present with the people. This was where people came to offer sacrifice and praise to the One inside the Temple. As ornate at Solomon's Temple was and as simple as the Second Temple came to be, the ordinary person was never allowed inside God's House.

"Worship" occurred in the home. There the head of the household (the father) took the responsibility to teach his family the laws and expectations of the LORD. He taught them to pray and honor God and others. In the home they learned the lessons of how to treat others fairly, to be humble enough to lift up the fallen, when to observe the special days of the LORD, and how to pray (talk) to God.

The primary home celebration occurred in the spring. This began in slavery as a somber meal with the family gathered around the table, eating in great haste for the Death Angel was about to spread its shadow over Egypt. Now, every spring this historic event was savored at the Seder Meal. It was (and is) a family affair, where a special menu, crafted into a symbolic journey, turns the dinner table into a sacred space. Bitter herbs, unleaven bread, and wine are blended into a liturgy of remembrance. Questions are asked by the youngest of the home and answered by the father. These include: Why is this night different from any other night? Why do we eat the unleavened bread and bitter herbs? Why do we dip green herbs in salt water? To each question the response (even though more elaborate answers are given) is "So we will remember." This event stood in direct opposition to the experience of the Temple. This worship experience was not about sacrifice but about remembering.

History tells us the path forward was not an easy path. The most striking event involved a Syrian king named Antiochus Epiphanes. When the Greeks took over the territory, Antiochus banned worship in the Temple and even brought in his own gods and sacrificed pigs on the altar. Since it was forbidden to openly teach Jewish history and religion, the people developed a simple yet ingenious game to continue the teaching process to their children. This was the Dreidel game. If, while teaching their children the scriptures, they heard the solders coming, they would hide the texts and pretend to be playing this game with a four-sided top. The daring revolt led by Judas Maccabeus recaptured the Temple and reinstated the worship process. It is said this absence of the centrality of the Temple was what created a renewal of religious fervor.

Eventually Rome took control of the territory, and Herod the Great came into power. Even though we have a profoundly negative view of Herod, he did some positive and creative things for the Jewish community. His claim to fame was two-fold. First, he was able to keep peace in the area for an extended period of time. Second, he loved to build. So, he approached the Jewish religious leaders with a plan to remodel and rebuild the Temple. The concept was not to regain the splendor of Solomon's Temple but to enlarge and enhance the courtyard area to make it more expansive. In the attempt to convince the religious leaders of the new plan, the major sticking point was the destruction of the Second Temple to construct a new Temple. Guaranteeing that the sacrificial process would not be interrupted, they agreed.

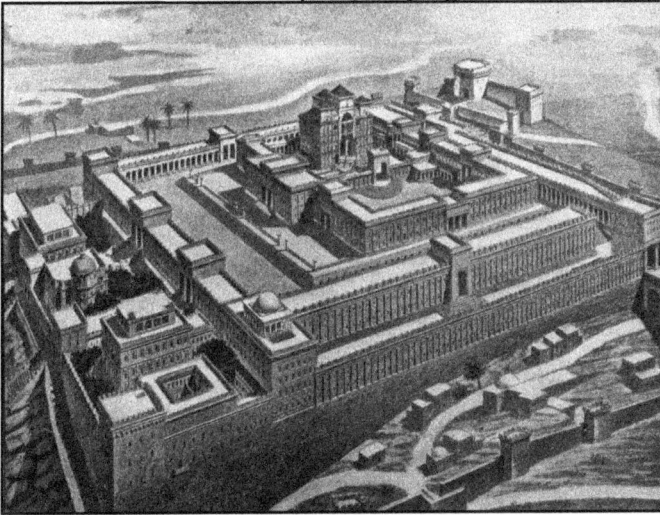

Herod's Temple (Pubic Domain Image)

The work, began in 19 B.C., was still in process when Jesus entered the space during that most holy of weeks. The area being raised and expanded, most visitors would now enter the courtyards from an entrance like a tunnel leading from the outside to the newly formed Court of the Gentiles. Looking more like a fortress, the holy mountain was converted into a large multi-level complex, eventually expanded to 1,600 feet by 900 feet and standing nine stories high with a massive wall 16 feet high. The interior was raised level-by-level again signifying that the higher worshiper, the more sacred the space.

The first space entered was the Court of the Gentiles—
a large area whose walls created the perimeter of the Temple.
This outer wall was comprised of covered areas called
porticos, where people and rabbis could gather to discuss
religious thought. This area may have more appropriately
resembled a county fair. Here animals were sold for
sacrifices, and Roman money (dirty money) was exchanged
for Temple money (clean money). This area was open to
anyone. Proselytes and interested persons could listen and
learn in the portico. As a person went deeper into the
complex, the rules changed. There were ten gates leading into
the Temple proper. Posted at each gate was a warning yo non-
Jews of the danger: "No foreigner is to enter within the
forecourt and the balustrade around the sanctuary. Whoever is
caught will have himself to blame for his subsequent death."

The next level was the Court of the Women. All Jews,
both male and female, could enter this space. This was the
place where cured lepers would report to the priest to get a
clean bill of health. Also, those who had completed a Nazarite
vow could get a haircut. Music (instrumental and vocal) and
dancing were experienced here.

The Court of the Israelites was for Jewish men
exclusively. Here they met with the Temple priests and
offered up their sacrifices of lambs, doves, and pigeons. The
small space was primarily a place of observation.

The innermost court was the Court of the Priests. Here
the actual sacrificial practice was completed. Animals offered
by the men were now sacrificed on the burning altar.

At the core of the complex stood the Temple proper.
Maintaining the Second Temple integrity, the Holy Place
contained the three primary appointments: the lamp stand, the
table of Showbread, and the Altar of Incense. Behind the

massive curtain separating the Holy Place and the Holy of Holies was the solitary "foundation stone."

Worship continued to be sacrificial, but over time the use of song and music became important in the process. The main function of the music was to accompany the procession leading to sacrifice. Richard C. Leonard notes:

> Israelite worship music was both vocal and instrumental; the sanctuary orchestra contributed to the celebration of Israel's covenant with the Lord. Its instruments fall into the same general classes with which we are familiar—percussion, winds (pipes), and strings. Horns, trumpets, cymbals, harps, and lyres were used when the ark was brought to Mount Zion, and their continued use is reflected in their mention in the Psalms. The sanctuary instruments were not solo instrument, but sounded simultaneously to call the assembly to worship (Psa. 98:6). Strings and pipes, if used, probably played the modalities (tune elements) in the psalm being sung, with perhaps distinctive patterns of ornamentation. Horns, trumpets and cymbals added to the festive joy by creating a larger sound. The selah of the Psalms may have been an instrumental interlude, or a "lifting up," of sound by both singers and instrumentalists. Tambourines, usually played by women, are mentioned in connection with dancing at Israelite festivals (Psa. 68:25) but were not used in the sanctuary where only men served as priests and musicians.[4]

The element of *deja vu* is experienced in Temple history. Just as the sons of Eli were less than honorable so became the office of High Priest. After the exile, the High Priest became the Chief Priest. Because of the loss of autonomy, Israel struggled against the outside forces to keep its religious heritage. The Chief Priest became the primary political and religious leader for the community. Once he became a Chief Priest, he held that position for life. Herod changed that concept and established an "elected" Chief Priest, he selected from the aristocratic Sadducee order. In this political climate, the Chief Priest was one who had to please Rome and simultaneously keep the Jewish community at peace.

Questions for Reflection

1) What was your response when you read that the Temple, in all its glory, was built with forced labor?

2) All the elaborate craftsmanship and splendor of the interior of the Temple was seen only by the priests and never by the common person. How do you think the Israelites felt when they realized they would only hear about the beauty of the Temple and not experience its beauty for themselves?

3) When the Temple was destroyed and many were carried to Babylon, the Israelites continued to practice their worship through devotion and prayer. How do you worship when you are away from your "Temple"?

4) When the people returned from exile the synagogues became a place not only worship but of study and community action. What does your worship community do to provide activities of learning and civic involvement?

5) The synagogue system instituted a liturgy of worship. The time of worship began with the celebrant (the person leading the worship) declaring, "In peace let us pray to the Lord." The people responded, "Lord, have mercy." What calls your community into the act of worship?

Endnotes

[1] Contemporary English Translation, American Bible Society, New York, 1995.

[2] A.Z. Idelsohn, Jewish Liturgy and Its Development, Dover Publications, Inc., New York, 1995. pg 22.

[3] B. Williams, and H. Anstall,; *Orthodox Worship: A Living Continuity with the Synagogue, the Temple and the Early Church*; Light and Life Publishing, Minneapolis, 1990.

[4] Richard C. Leonard, Music and Worship in the Bible. Laudemont Ministries, Hamilton, Illinois.

Chapter 4

First to the Jew — Then to All the World
Shifts That Changed History

By the time Jesus arrived, the Jewish world had changed from its simple wilderness belief system into an arena where there were three primary theologies at work. The Sadducees were, for lack of a better term, "old school." They held tight to the teachings of the Torah (The Books of Moses); they had a deep love and respect for the Temple; and they resisted the notion of angels, demons, and an after-life. They believed that if the Temple were honored and maintained, no one would be able to destroy the Jewish community.

The Sadducees seemed to be comprised of the nobility of the Jewish community. With their personal interest at stake, they found measures of compromise with Rome which controlled the territory. It appears that from their ranks arose the formation of the Sanhedrin. Rome had offered the Jewish community a very special privilege allowing them to maintain their own religion and religious practices. The cost was peace. As long as the Jewish community paid their taxes and kept peace among themselves, all was well. But, Rome also held the threat over their heads that if they caused Rome trouble or embarrassment, Rome would bring its full force upon them and turn the nation into dust.

The Pharisees were progressive in nature. They loved the words of the law and the prophets, which spawned great debates of interpretation. They had a deep-seated belief in angels, demons, and receiving of justice in the after-life. Unlike the Sadducees who denounced the mystical and heavenly, the Pharisees embraced the belief in reward and punishment when a person crosses over from the mortal to the immortal. From this description one begins to recognize why this group was most often found in the presence of Jesus— who also spent much of his time on earth reinterpreting the old law and who spoke often of the rewards and punishments in the after-life.

The Essenes were the mystics. They separated themselves from the rest of the society and focused on the teachings revealed to the Teacher of Righteousness. They claimed knowledge of the "true law" and often used apocalyptic imagery placing themselves as Sons of Light living in the midst of the Sons of Darkness. It is thought that after the death of Zechariah and Elizabeth, John the Baptizer was raised and nurtured by this community. Thus his fiery cries and pointed proclamations were versed in the vocabulary of the Essenes.

It is into this religious culture Jesus appeared into a world filled with religious and political tensions. The primary places of worship remained: Temple, synagogue, and home. Hayyim Schauss[1] notes that by the beginning of the Common Era, the Sabbath had established itself as a ritual observance in its own right. Special meals were prepared, and often people would wear their best clothes to the services in the synagogue. In other words, they began the tradition of what we would call eating "Sunday Lunch" and dressing up in "Sunday clothes." Late Friday afternoon the priest would ascent the tower of the Temple or go to the roof of an elevated house and blow a trumpet six times to signal the arrival of the Sabbath day. The families would gather for the meal, which began the day.

One must note that the Jewish concept of "day" is not the current Western perception. In Western thought we arise to a new day, work, and the rest from our labors. In this culture they began the day when three stars were visible.

They enjoyed a meal and then rested—which led to one's work being the concluding act of the day.

Reading through the Gospels, one notes that Jesus is often found celebrating the Sabbath meal and attending the Sabbath synagogue services. From the beginning of Jesus' ministry, he pushed against the limits of the comfortable. In Luke, Jesus attended his hometown synagogue.

> *When he came to Nazareth, where he had been brought up, he went to the synagogue on the sabbath day, as was his custom. He stood up to read, and the scroll of the prophet Isaiah was given to him. He unrolled the scroll and found the place where it was written: 'The Spirit of the Lord is upon me, because he has anointed me to bring good news to the poor. He has sent me to proclaim release to the captives and recovery of sight to the blind, to let the oppressed go free, to proclaim the year of the Lord's favour.' And he rolled up the scroll, gave it back to the attendant, and sat down. The eyes of all in the synagogue were fixed on him. Then he began to say to them, 'Today this scripture has been fulfilled in your hearing.' All spoke well of him and were amazed at the gracious words that came from his mouth.* (Luke 4:16-22 NRSV)[2]

When Jesus worshiped in a synagogue, a Sabbath worship pattern had become established. There was a five-part service comprised of the offering of prayers, the singing of the psalm, the blessings, the readings from the Scriptures, and a commentary on the sacred passage of the day. No official clergy was appointed to oversee the services—elders and teachers would share the responsibility. On this day the leaders in the Nazareth synagogue offered the task of reading the scripture to the home-town boy—Jesus. Apparently, this was well into the service for the text entered the service at the reading of the scripture. Jesus followed the reading with his commentary on the text.

In Jerusalem, Jesus taught from the portico of the Court of the Gentiles. He was challenged by the authorities in the Court of the Women when they brought an adulterous woman to be judged. We understand he paid his Temple Tax. What we do not experience is Jesus entering the Court of the Israelites to offer sacrifices even though the Temple continued to be primarily a place of sacrifice.

The Temple exploded with life at the festival of Pesach or Passover. Jerusalem was literally packed corner-to-corner with people during this spring festival. The ancient ones often said that a great miracle occurred every year since all who visited Jerusalem had a place to lay their heads and rest.

During "ordinary" time there was a single station in the Temple to process the sacrifices. At Passover there were twenty-four sacrificial stations. As the day of Passover approached, the men moved toward the Temple for three flights of sacrifices—the first beginning around three o'clock in the afternoon. Those bringing their sheep would slaughter the animal themselves and then present the sacrifice to a priest who would take it and lift it up to God. During the processing of the sacrifice, the Levitical Priests would sing Psalms of Praise accompanied by musical instruments. Those bringing the sacrifice stood in the Court of the Israelites and prayed. The entire company of sacrificial offerings would be processed in about a three-hours span. Those who brought the lamb would then return home with the sacrificed animal wrapped in its own skin.

The Passover celebration was the one festival celebrated in the home. On this special night everyone was expected to gather at a Passover table. The rich would invite the poor into their homes, and almost anywhere there was a gathering place, people gathered to celebrate.

It is in the home worship setting Jesus began to restructure worship for a soon-to-be-born community. The Seder Meal, or the Passover Feast, was very structured by the Jesus' time. Years of tradition had fashioned the liturgy of the evening into a pattern not to be tampered with or changed. The meal centered around symbolic food and glasses of wine.

What follows is a very simplified pattern of the Seder meal:

The gathering of the family and the singing of joyous songs.
The lighting of the candles of home (by the female head of the
    household).
The pouring and drinking of the first cup of wine representing
    God's declaration freedom saying, "I am the Lord, and I
    will free you from the burdens of the Egyptians."
The eating of green herbs symbolizing new life.
The pouring and drinking of the second cup of wine
    representing God's promise that "I will deliver you from
    bondage."
The eating of bitter herbs symbolized the remembrance of the
    bitterness of slavery. And the hasty eating of the Matzah
    (unleavened bread).
There are four questions to be asked by the youngest child in
    the house and answered by the head of the household.
    These are the questions:
        "Why is this night different from all other nights?"
        "On other nights we eat all kinds of herbs, but on this
        night we eat only bitter herbs. Why?"
        "On all other nights, we do not dip herbs at all. Why
        do we dip them tonight?"
        "Why do we dine tonight with special ceremony?"
Pouring the third cup of wine and its drinking symbolized the
    third divine promise "I will redeem you with an
    outstretched arm."

Now dinner was served, and unleavened bread was eaten at
the beginning and ending of the meal so that the entire
meal is sandwiched between the symbols to remind them
of the years of slavery in Egypt.
The fourth cup of wine was poured and drunk, noting that "our
salvation is not complete."
They remember God's promise, "And I will take you to be my
people."
The Passover celebration ended with a blessing and a song.

When Jesus and the disciples gathered in the upper
room for their meal, there must have been looks of shock and
disbelief as Jesus, apparently in the posture of the head of the
household, began to change the liturgy of the meal. It is quite
possible, as one reads the account of this meal in the Gospels
of Matthew, Mark, and Luke, that the loaf of bread Jesus
broke was the matzah, eaten in haste after the second cup of
wine. Jesus shifted the symbolism from that of slavery to that
of sacrifice as he says, *"Take, eat, this is my body"* (Matthew
26:26 NRSV). If this were not enough to cause the disciples
to question (even within their own hearts) the reason for the
change, Jesus then truly shocked them as he took a cup of
wine and declared, *"Drink from it, all of you; for this is my
blood of the covenant which is poured out for many for the
forgiveness of sins"* (Matthew 26:28 NRSV). If this is true,
the cup of wine Jesus lifted up before the disciples was the
third cup—the Cup of Redemption.

This brings into clarity the event in the Garden. Jesus
prayed that the "cup" be taken away. Jesus realized that true
redemption cannot occur without the shedding of blood. The
Redeemer lifted up the Cup of Redemption.

After the resurrection we find Jesus commissioning the
disciples:
So when they had come together, they asked him,

'Lord, is this the time when you will restore the kingdom to Israel?' He replied, 'It is not for you to know the times or periods that the Father has set by his own authority. But you will receive power when the Holy Spirit has come upon you; and you will be my witnesses in Jerusalem, in all Judea and Samaria, and to the ends of the earth.' When he had said this, as they were watching, he was lifted up, and a cloud took him out of their sight. (Luke 1: 6-9 NRSV)

Two things of note. First, the disciples were still concerned with the restoration of the Kingdom of Israel—and after all, was that not the task of the Messiah? Second, Jesus did not instruct the disciples to go out and create a new religion, denomination, or sect. Jesus said to go and be witnesses. And what are they to be witness about? The message of Jesus (i.e., the gospel or good news) and the power of the God of the Jewish community. So the first "church" was not a separate entity but was attached to the Jewish faith. The followers of The Way, the first name for the community who followed Jesus as Messiah, were good Jews. They obeyed the law. They attended synagogue and Temple. They were Jewish followers of Jesus as Messiah.

If left alone, this new cult would become just another group added to the Essenes, Pharisees, and Sadducees. But that was not the case. In Acts we read how the followers of Jesus were very vocal in public—especially as they ventured into the Temple courtyards proclaiming that Jesus was the Messiah. We read of the arrests and imprisonment of the Apostles and how early in the birthing of this new community they concerned themselves with the welfare of all—which echoed the call of the prophets.

It was the great Gamaliel who attempted to call a halt to the arresting of the disciples of Jesus. In Acts 5 we read how the Sadducees arrested the apostles and threw them into prison. During the night the angel of the Lord opened the doors of the prison, and they all walked out. And, true to their nature, they appeared again the next day in the Temple. The Sadducees wanted to end the controversy by killing the apostles, but Gamaliel responded:

> *Then he said to them, "Fellow Israelites, consider carefully what you propose to do to these men. For some time ago Theudas rose up, claiming to be somebody, and a number of men, about four hundred, joined him; but he was killed, and all who followed him were dispersed and disappeared. After him Judas the Galilean rose up at the time of the census and got people to follow him; he also perished, and all who followed him were scattered. So in the present case, I tell you, keep away from these men and let them alone; because if this plan or this undertaking is of human origin, it will fail; but if it is of God, you will not be able to overthrow them—in that case you may even be found fighting against God!"* (Acts 5:35-39 NRSV)

The followers would worship in their traditional Jewish settings beginning Friday evening through Saturday evening. On Sunday, the first day of the week, they gathered to share a memorial meal and tell the stories of Jesus. It would be nice to think the Jewish authorities would now leave the new group alone, but that was not the case. They exercised the right of religious authority tolerated by Rome and began to purge those "corrupting" the true religion. The major shift came when a highly trained Pharisee, who was on a mission to arrest those trouble-makers, had an encounter with Jesus himself. Paul, a Pharisee trained by Gamaliel, changed the make-up of the community by inviting those who were not Jewish to become "believers."

Soon conflict arose between the Jewish Church comprised of Jewish believers and Paul's Gentile Church of outsiders. The question at hand was "Would the new converts be required to become Jewish first to become Christian?" In 51 AD, the conflict reached a point where some resolve must be made. That resolution came in what is called the Jerusalem Council recorded in Acts 15.

> *Then certain individuals came down from Judea and were teaching the brothers, "Unless you are circumcised according to the custom of Moses, you cannot be saved." And after Paul and Barnabas had no small dissension and debate with them, Paul and Barnabas and some of the others were appointed to go up to Jerusalem to discuss this question with the apostles and the elders. ... James replied, "My brothers, listen to me. Simeon has related how God first looked favorably on the Gentiles, to take from among them a people for his name. This agrees with the words of the prophets, as it is written, 'After this I will return, and I will rebuild the dwelling of David, which has fallen; from its ruins I will rebuild it, and I will set it up, so that all other peoples may seek the Lord— even all the Gentiles over whom my name has been called. Thus says the Lord, who has been making these things known from long ago.' Therefore I have reached the decision that we should not trouble those Gentiles who are turning to God, but we should write to them to abstain only from things polluted by idols and from fornication and from whatever has been strangled and from blood. For in every city, for generations past, Moses has had those who proclaim him, for he has been read aloud every sabbath in the synagogues." (Acts 15: 1-2, 13b-21)*

So the Council agreed the requirements for those Gentile believers would be very simple—turn away from idolatry and fornication and refrain from eating blood and animals which were strangled. Their task was to gather and tell the stories of Jesus and believe.

Twenty years later, Rome came down on Jerusalem with full force destroying the Temple and the city driving away all the inhabitants. The Jerusalem Church was dispersed. But what remained intact were those Gentile communities of believers now identified by the name "Christian."

We do find in the book of Acts that the Church had the beginning of a structured liturgy. They would sing songs, offer prayers, and tell the stories of Jesus. Someone would "preach" or expound upon the story of the day, and, finally, they celebrated the remembrance meal.

They also had an order for those who serve. In Acts 11 one finds the distinction of *elder*. The underlying word is the Greek word *presbuterous*. This designation was recorded as far back as Moses, who chose elders to be the decision makers. Here the same context was established. These "wisdom keepers" found favor among the believers because of their experience. In Acts 13 the tasks are broadened to include prophets and teachers. Acts 21 establishes those who reach out to the world—the evangelist.

Emperor Nero was in power when Paul arrived in Rome to await his trial. The historical event of the burning of Rome is clouded by the mythical story of Nero "fiddling" from the roof-top. Historians tell us approximately 75 percent of Rome burned. The 25 percent which remained was inhabited by the birthing Christian community. This gave Nero the perfect "out" to blame the fire on the Christians. Nero put to death the two major figures of Christianity—Paul and Peter. Along with the loss of their voices of authority, the Christians were now being tracked down, arrested, and subjected to torture and tormented. Because of the fury of Nero, the Church went underground for safety.

The historian Tacitus wrote in his work Annals concerning the persecution of the Christians:

> Nero fastened the guilt and inflicted the most exquisite tortures on a class hated for their abominations, called Christians ... an immense multitude was convicted, not so much of the crime of firing the city, as of hatred against mankind. Mockery of every sort was added to their deaths. Covered with the skins of beasts, they were torn by dogs and perished, or were nailed to crosses, or were doomed to the flames and burnt, to serve as a nightly illumination, when daylight had expired.[3]

Rome thought this action would destroy the new community. These events of torture led Rome to believe that these acts would discourage anyone from becoming a part of the Christian community. But those taken captive boldly accepted their fates and, instead of becoming examples of criminal punishment, became praised as martyrs, whose courage provided a magnetic pull drawing others toward the Church.

Without getting into the step-by-step, community-by-community expanse of the church, two things are evident. First, the stronghold of Christianity now stood outside the Jewish homeland. And second, these were "pagans" who struggled with the new ideals and concepts of Jesus as Messiah (since they had no previous concept of the Messianic purpose). They did not have Bibles. There were no rule books to follow. And the one person who provided the foundational leadership was the itinerant Paul. For all practical purposes, these churches were "making it up as they go." And that was what Paul struggled against—churches, spread out across the region, each with its own idea of what Christianity should be. And now that voice was silent.

The "church" gathered primarily in homes, although there were areas where they would find larger gathering places, which were isolated and safe. Without the Jewish influence, the Church now claimed Sunday, the first day of the week and the resurrection day, as their day of worship. And, being in a different culture, the concept of the day beginning at dusk shifted to the idea that "day" began at sunrise. So the primary function of worship was to gather and celebrate Easter every Sabbath day. And the Sabbath day was given a new name—the Lord's Day.

To say the church became invisible during the years of persecution is a misnomer. The persecutions were not constant, and there were times when the community could be public in its posture. They were visible even to the authorities. Pliny the Younger, whose real name was Gaius Caecilius Cilo (61 AD 112 AD), wrote hundreds of letters and articles. He was not only an author but also a lawyer and magistrate of Ancient Rome. He was not sure whether the Christians deserved the criminal status placed upon them. As he arrested Christians he would question them concerning their rites and rituals. Apparently his information never came from faithful Christians but from those who had left the ranks of the Christian community. From their reports he recorded their worship practices as follows:

> they were accustomed to meet on a fixed day before dawn and sing responsively a hymn to Christ as to a god, and to bind themselves by oath, not to some crime, but not to commit fraud, theft, or adultery, not falsify their trust, nor to refuse to return a trust when called upon to do so. When this was over, it was their custom to depart and to assemble again to partake of foodbut ordinary and innocent food. [4]

Even though the Christians were hunted and persecuted, they were ever present in the empire. With the threat of arrest, the community began to create ways of identifying each other. The most prominent was making a sign of a fish—the first symbol of the new community. It is said that when Christians were talking to others they perceived as a fellow Christians, they would make an arch in the dust with their foot. If the others were indeed Christians, they would make a corresponding arch to form the outline of a fish. This "symbol" was also their affirmation of faith. The Greek word is ichthus, a five-letter acronym for Jesus-Christ-God's-Son-Savior.

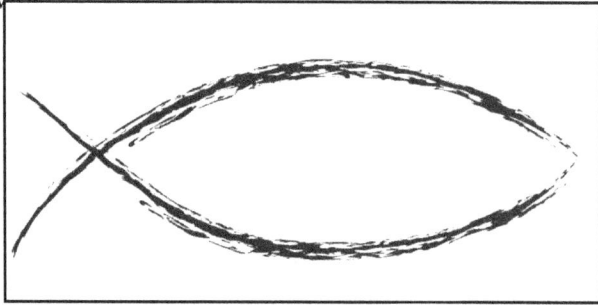

Very little is known about the true nature of worship among the various Christian communities simply because they were secretive in nature. Justin Martyr recorded actions of the church which existed around 155 AD. These included baptism, the Eucharistic meal, Sunday assembly, the reading of the "memoirs of the apostles" (by this date copies of the Gospels were in circulation), and the teaching from the scriptures. This was presented by "the president" who was seated while all the other people stood.

There was evidence of two distinct worship services. The first was a service of prayer, word, and fellowship, open to all. The second service celebrated the Eucharistic meal, open only to "church members."

There are accounts of the developing of order and liturgy by the end of the second century. In 1753 a document was discovered by Philtheos Bryennios, a Greek Bishop of Nicomedia. The document dates from around 175 AD and is titled *The Didache* (pronounced "dee-dah-khay") or *The Lord's Teaching Through The Twelve Apostles to the Nations*. There are sixteen "chapters," or units, which give direction to the early church. Sections address topics such as which sins are to be forgiven and which cannot be forgiven, response to false teachers, food offered to idols, the leadership within the church, reception of new members, support for the prophets and teachers, when to assemble for worship, and a call to watchfulness for the "coming of the Lord."

Chapters seven through ten specifically address worship elements.

Chapter Seven
And concerning baptism, in this manner baptize: when you have gone over these things, baptize in the name of the Father, and the Son, and the Holy Spirit, in running water. If you do not have running water, baptize in other water. If you are not able to use cold water, use warm. And if you have neither, pour water on the head three times, in the name of the Father, the Son, and the Holy Spirit. ....

Chapter Eight
And let not your fasts be with those of the hypocrites, for they fast on Mondays and Thursdays, but you fast Wednesdays and Fridays. Do not pray as the hypocrites but as the Lord commanded in His gospel. Pray like this: Our Father in heaven, hallowed is Your name, Your kingdom come and Your will be done on earth as it is in heaven. Give us our daily bread for today and forgive our debts as we forgive those who owe us.

Please do not lead us into a test, but deliver us from the evil one. For You have the power and the glory forever. Pray like this three times a day.

Chapter Nine
Concerning the Eucharist (communion) give thanks like this: First for the cup: We give thanks to You, our Father, for Your holy vine of David, Your servant, which You made known to us through Jesus, Your Servant. Glory to You forever.
Concerning the broken bread: We give thanks to You, our Father, for the life and knowledge that You made known to us through Jesus, Your Servant. Glory to You forever. As this broken bread was scattered over the hills and was brought together becoming one, so gather Your Church from the ends of the earth into Your kingdom, for You have all power and glory forever through Jesus Christ.
Do not let anyone eat or drink of your Eucharist meal except the ones who have been baptized into the name of the Lord. For the Lord said concerning this: "do not give that which is holy to the dogs."

Chapter Ten
After you are filled, give thanks like this: We thank you, Holy Father, for Your Holy name which you made to dwell in our hearts, and for knowledge and faith and immortality as You made known to us through Jesus, Your Servant. Glory to You forever. ... Let grace come and this world pass away. Hosanna to the Son of David! If anyone is holy, let him come. If anyone is not, let him repent. Maranatha (Lord come). Amen. [5]

By 200 AD specific liturgies were used within the church. Hippolytus recorded the liturgy for the Eucharistic meal, which included words and actions the church continues

to use to this day. These included the familiar:
>**Celebrant:** The Lord be with you.
>**Response:** And with your spirit.
>**Celebrant:** Lift up your hearts.
>**Response:** We have them with the Lord.
>**Celebrant:** Let us give thanks unto the Lord.
>**Response:** It is fitting and right.

And the benediction:
>In God the Father Almighty. Amen.
>And in the Lord Jesus Christ. Amen.
>And in the Holy Spirit in the Holy Church. Amen.

The church remained in hiding until around 312 AD.

The event which lifted the seclusion was brought about by the shifting of power within the Roman Empire. Two powerful men, Constantine and Maximinus, were posturing themselves to become the next emperor. What follows is only one version of the events leading to the Battle of Milvian Bridge. Being troubled the day before the battle, Constantine entered his tent and began praying to the Roman sun god. During his prayer he saw a blinding light and within that light two Greek letters—chi (X) and rho (P) superimposed over each other. Then he heard a voice declaring, "With this sign you will conquer." He immediately went out and instructed his soldiers to put the symbol on their shields and armor. And, as history records, under *that* sign he was victorious.

Being informed that these letters were the first two letters of the Greek word for Christ, he acknowledged the power splendor of Christianity, and suddenly the church "underground" came out of hiding.

Questions for Reflection

1) When Jesus worshiped in the synagogue he participated by reading scripture and teaching a lesson from the text of the day. Jesus was not a Jewish priest but a lay person. How is the laity involved in your worship service?

2) The Passover Seder was the most sacred time for the Jewish household and was celebrated as a family. What is the most sacred holy-day observed in your home?

3) At the Jerusalem Council, as recorded in Acts 15, the requirements for a Gentile to become a Christian were established. The "rules" were that they should abstain from eating food which had been presented to idols, the consuming of blood, eating anything which had been strangled, and they must not commit any sexual sin. Does your community have prescribed "rules" to be obeyed as precursors to being accepted as part of the Christian community?

4) Pliny the Younger noted the strange behavior which set the people called Christians apart from the rest of society through the singing of hymns, holding each other to a higher standard

of living by not committing fraud, theft, or adultery, and partaking in a special meal. What sets your faith community apart from the "outside" world?

5) The early Christian community created symbols as a way of identifying believers such as the Ichthus or fish. What symbols are used in your worship/faith community to declare an allegiance to Christ?

Endnotes

[1] Hayyim Schauss, The Jewish Festivals: A Guide to Their History and Observance, "Chapter 2: Sabbath in its development." Union of American Hebrew Congregations, 1966.)

[2] New Revised Standard Version Bible, Nation Council of Churches, United States, 1989.

[3] Tacitus, Annals, Book 15, Section 44.

[4] Pliny the Younger, *Letters*, 10.96.

[5] Text of the Didache.

Chapter 5

From the House to the Cathedral
Building Worship (313 AD - 1517 AD)

It is 313 AD as the dust settles down upon a unified empire. Constantine emerged as victor. In consultation with Licinius, Constantine constructed *The Edict of Milan* and pronounced it across the empire.

> When I, Constantine Augustus, as well as I, Licinius Augustus, fortunately met near Mediolanurn (Milan), and were considering everything that pertained to the public welfare and security, we thought, among other things which we saw would be for the good of many, those regulations pertaining to the reverence of the Divinity ought certainly to be made first, so that we might grant to the Christians and others full authority to observe that religion which each preferred; whence any Divinity whatsoever in the seat of the heavens may be propitious and kindly disposed to us and all who are placed under our rule. ... Therefore, your Worship [Bishop of the Christian Church] should know that it has pleased us to remove all conditions whatsoever, which were in the rescripts formerly given to you officially, concerning the Christians and now any one of these who wishes to observe Christian religion may do so freely and openly, without molestation. We thought it fit to commend these things most fully to your care that you may know that we have given to those Christians free and unrestricted opportunity of religious worship. ... And since these Christians are known to have possessed not only those places in which they were accustomed to assemble, but also other property, namely the churches, belonging to them

as a corporation and not as individuals, all these things which we have included under the above law, you will order to be restored, . . . Moreover, in order that the statement of this decree of our good will may come to the notice of all, this rescript, published by your decree, shall be announced everywhere and brought to the knowledge of all, so that the decree of this, our benevolence, cannot be concealed.

Later, in 321 AD, Constantine declared Sunday to be a legal holiday or, as he described it, "the day of the sun." He intended the day to acknowledge or honor the god Mithras, the Unconquered Sun. This day of rest also coincided with the "first day of the week" celebrated by the Christian community as a "little Easter."

The leniency of Constantine allowed the Church, for the first time *in toto*, freely and openly to worship and evangelize. One might imagine the sudden emergence of an organized church in its splendor and unity to enter this new opportunity prepared to take on the world—but that did not happened. The church had been scattered and disjointed. Without the ability to openly communicate and hold dialog concerning theology and scripture, the church of Constantine's time looked similar to the church of today—not in appearance but in the fragmentary concepts which separate the many Protestant denominations of the current era. Now, as then, the unifying element centers around the life, death, and resurrection of Jesus. But beyond those foundations are theological issues which isolate and polarize. How are the scriptures to be interpret? As hand-written by God or as a guide book to be reinterpreted by each generation? How is baptism to be conducted? Is one required to be completely submerged under water, or, as the old hair-cream commercial said, will "a little dab'l do ya"? And who is "eligible" to receive the elements of the Lord's Supper? Only church

members? Only members of a particular church? Anyone
who acknowledges Jesus as Lord and Savior?

It was immediately evident that there were differing
views and values. Some of these beliefs and doctrines began
to tear at the very fabric of the church. The infighting over the
rightness and wrongness was so strong that the emperor called
a meeting of all the bishops of the church to come to Nicea
and "hash out" the dividing issues. One major issue was the
the fracturous views of Arianism that denied the sonship of
Jesus. The outcome of the Council was twofold. First, the
Council developed a definition for the "who" of Jesus and his
relationship with God. Eusebius used the word *homoousious,*
meaning "of one substance." This concept of Jesus and God
being of one substance was definitive in placing Jesus as both
fully human and completely divine. Many sources give credit
to the Early Church Father Origin, but this is due only to the
fact he used the word in his writings.

Now that the Church had a definition for the
personhood of Jesus, thus placing Arianism outside as
heretical, the next step was to create a theological statement
with which to unify the church. The result was the
construction of the Nicene Creed. As one reads this statement
of faith and theology, it is apparent the purpose is to create a
fence around the faith. The original text of 325 AD was
expanded for clarification in 381 AD to read as follows. (I
have placed bold emphasis for the purpose of creating a visual
image of the theological progression.)

> We believe in one **God, the Father** Almighty, Maker
> of heaven and earth, and of all things visible and
> invisible.
> And in one Lord **Jesus Christ, the onlybegotten Son
> of God**, begotten of the Father before all worlds, **Light
> of Light, very God of very God, begotten, not made,
> being of one substance with the Father**; by whom all

things were made; who for us men, and for our
salvation, came down from heaven, and was **incarnate
by the Holy Ghost of the Virgin Mary**, and **was
made man**; he was **crucified for us** under Pontius
Pilate, and suffered, and was buried, and **the third day
he rose again**, according to the Scriptures, and
ascended into heaven, and sitteth on the right hand of
the Father; from thence he shall come again, with
glory, to judge the quick and the dead; whose kingdom
shall have no end.
And in the **Holy Ghost, the Lord and Giver of life,**
who proceedeth from the Father, who **with the Father
and the Son together is worshiped** and glorified, who
spake by the prophets.
In one **holy catholic and apostolic Church**; we
acknowledge **one baptism** for the remission of sins;
we look for the **resurrection of the dead**, and the **life
of the world** to come. Amen [1]

With the Christian community free to worship openly,
a major shift occurred as they moved from small house
church/communities to a place where large crowds could
gather. The Jewish community had embraced a Greco-Roman
building, originally designed for worshiping their gods and for
receptions, funerals, and civic functions. The Christians, who
needed a "synagogue," modified the Byzantine architectural
style into a house of Christian worship—the basilica.

Dr. Robbin Gibbons, a lecturer at the University of
Oxford (England), notes these particular characteristics:
    The basic feature of this building was a lofty
    rectangular hall. ... As a rule the roof was either a flat
    wooden ceiling or an open timber roof. ... The focal
    point of the building was the semicircular apse where
    the bishop had his seat (cathedra) and were the
    presbyters sat round him. ... The altar table was

usually positioned close to this end (as) the bishop and senior clergy were ranged behind it for the Eucharist and other main services ... The shape of the hall was rectangular, the main space divided into three; the nave and two side isles. Here the lower clergy, the choir, and the people gathered. [2]

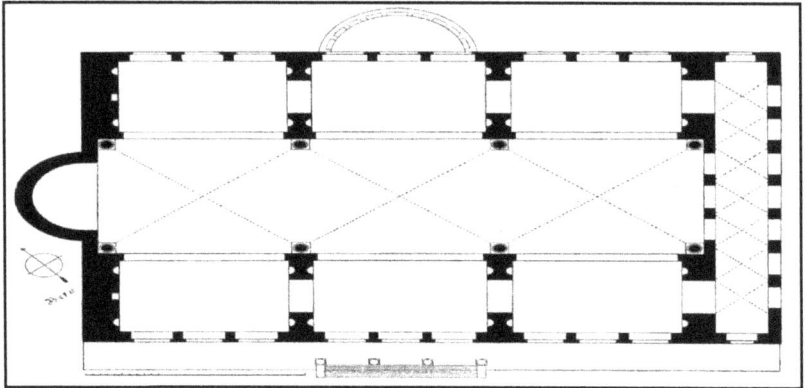

Basilica Floor Plan (Public Domain Image)

As these structures sprang up across the empire, there arose a practice of constructing the basilica over the graves of the saints. Thus begins the relationship between cemeteries and the church.

The church was thick-walled, tall and had small windows. In an attempt to "brighten up" the space several concepts were instituted. Artistic representations of Christian scenes were depicted on elaborate tapestries and paintings. It may have been in the darkness of the basilica where the concept of candles on the altar table began. We often think these lights represent the presence of Christ, the light of the world. In reality, the practice began because the clergy needed light to read the liturgy. In the fourth century the Paschal, or Christ Candle, was introduced during the Easter season.

In this time period the sacred meal moved out of the

house and into the church. With that move, its observance shifted from the "pot luck" around the kitchen table to a sacred mystery to be administered by the now professional clergy. The meal had previously been a full meal with elements of "remembrance" inserted. Now the service was called the Eucharist or Holy Communion and brought with it an element of awe and mystery. It was no longer bread and wine but a holy and sacred transformed sacrament.

The structure of the building, the sacredness of the meal, and the larger gathering of the community also gave rise to the desire to standardize the liturgy (the way worship is conducted). Rites and rituals were developed to address the special needs of the community. Latin became the language of worship so as to assimilate the church into the culture. Feast days were established, and the "Christian" year was divided into celebratory units or seasons: (1) Christmas, Epiphany, and the feast of the saints and (2) Easter and its feasts.

Early in the life of the church, images of Jesus attached to the cross appeared. This was not a primary image of the underground church, which seemed more attached to the resurrection and life rather than the pain and death of Jesus. When the image of the crucified Christ rose as the central focus of the worship space, the practice of using the hand to make the sign of the cross at times of worship and prayer began to be used in the church and wherever they found themselves in a posture of prayer and worship.

As the church was now being led by professional clergy, the identifying clothes, or vestments, began to separate the priests from the laity. This concept is not new. The same process of "priestly garb" was created with the construction of the Tabernacle. Initially, the clergy wore simple white robes called "alb." By the fifth century the custom was for the bishops to wear purple. From this beginning, the clerical dress became more and more elaborate.

The worship space was open with the exception of the Bishop's chair, the seats for the clergy, the Altar (used to hold the sacred meal elements), and a baptismal font. As the people stood around the basilica, the bishop would pray and preach seated from his chair. Fountains were often placed near the entrance of the basilica so those entering could enter "clean." And the baptismal font held cold water to be poured over the body of the infant or the head of an adult. By the Middle Ages this process had evolved to "sprinkling," which may have come out of necessity rather than choice. Those were dark, cold spaces, and the last thing one would want was to catch a cold or get sick from being wet.

Processionals began with the bringing in of lights followed by the clergy. There were chants offered with antiphonal responses from the gathered of "Amen," "Maranatha," or "Alleluia." The worship experience was also enhanced by the singing of solos—usually sung during the administration of the Eucharistic meal.

The vessels used to serve the meal changed. In the home church the vessels were small and simple. Now with the gathering of larger numbers, the vessels were enlarged to provide for the additional servings. These elements of bread and wine were in clear view. The practice of covering the elements with white linen came later. This was not to shroud the bread and wine in mystery but rather to keep the flies and insects out/off. Therefore, the liturgical practice of covering the elements, like the lights on the altar, developed out of a practical need, not a theological mandate.

In the eighth century an architectural shift occurred. Now the preferred style was Romanesque—a three-storied building with massive pillars, large supportive arches, and colorful interiors. Windows were very small and few in number. The stained glass window was appearing in many churches, showering the interior with vibrant colors. The windows of red, blue, yellow, and green would blend to blanket the worship service in a mantle of purple. The identifying characteristic of the Romanesque church was the round arches used inside and outside the structure. There was also a floor plan shift as the church's form resembled a cross or cruciform. A choir loft was added to lead chants.

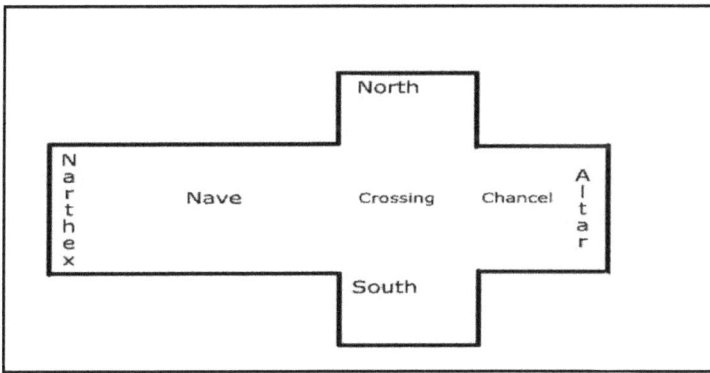

Romanesque Cruciform Floor Plan (Public Domain Image)

The altar was moved from the center and placed against the eastern wall. On the chancel, or sacred area, a pulpit was added. Words from the bishop or priest were no longer offered sitting down but standing up. The result was the pulpit became the liturgical center of worship. This move brings to mind two points of interest. The first point has to do with the liturgical vestments of the priest. They became very ornate, and the priest often wore a chasuble (the cape style vestment worn over the alb), decorated on the back side with a peacock of brilliant colors. The peacock had been used to symbolize the death and resurrection event. The bird would lose all its feathers and then, in short time, would regrow a new set of feathers in all their splendor. When the priest would lift up the elements in the Great Thanksgiving, spreading his arms, the bird would come to life with its bold colors.

The second event happened within the Great Thanksgiving. The liturgy, in Latin, would arrive at the place where the priest would declare the mysterious words "This is my body"—*hoc est corpus (meum)*. At this point in history, the people thought something magical was happening to the bread and wine as the priest, facing the stone wall, would cry out these words. The words echoing throughout the church became confused by those not understanding Latin. The common people arrived at their own interpretation of the mysterious actions of the priest declaring *hoc est corpus* a magical spell changing one thing into something else. Thus was born the magical phrase "Hocus Pocus." This is also said to be the catalyst for a familiar children's song, *The Hokey-Pokey*. Historians say the children sang the song in a mocking manner to describe the actions of the priest during the eucharistic prayer which included the rubic of hands up, hands down, and turning around.

During the time of the Latin rite, the common person struggled to make sense of what was the correct moral posture of a Christian. As a way of bringing the "message" out from a distant language, drama was incorporated as a supplement to worship. The origin of these plays was thought to be the monks of the Dominican and Franciscan orders. At first, simple plays were performed to educate the people and better inform them regarding the sermons being preached. In the thirteenth century the simplicity moved to a deeper level, using actors and theatrical elements. At first, small and simple, the art grew into primary pageants celebrating the holy seasons. Passion plays were created around the Lenten and Easter seasons as well as the Advent and Christmas times.

By this time many churches had created written liturgies so there could a continuity between the churches regarding worship patterns and practices. Elaborate volumes termed *Book of Hours* gave guidance to not only the primary Sabbath worship but also the activities and worship times throughout the day and week. Typically the book's contents were ordered as follows: a calendar of Church feasts, excerpts from each of the four gospels, the Little Office of the Blessed Virgin Mary, the fifteen Psalms of Degrees, the seven Penitential Psalms, a Litany of Saints, an Office for the Dead, the Hours of the Cross, a number of various prayers. These books were not simply guides but were works of art.

Image of 14th century Book of Hours (Public Domain)

The service had lost its "home setting"and was now ordered and developed. The central focus of the worship event was the Eucharist with a designed liturgy. The worship event now follows this structure:

Introit - opening of the worship service, either spoken or sung

Kyrie - a prayer: "Lord, have mercy; Christ, have mercy; Lord, have mercy."

Greeting - acknowledging those present

Collect - a short prayer for the day.

Epistle - reading
Psalmody - Psalms put to music, sung or chanted by the choir
Gospel - a reading from one of the Gospel
Presentation of Gifts
Chant over the Gifts
Prayer over the Gifts
Eucharistic Prayer
Lord's Prayer
The Peace
Communion - reception of the Eucharist
Dismissal - a sending forth

Underlying these worship developments were the new-found power and influence the church had gained. It was no longer a floundering flock but a force to be reckoned with. I will not address those issues of political and social power. These were primarily dynamics taking place outside the worship space. However, I will mention the Great Schism of 1054 AD, which separated the unified Catholic church into Eastern and Western divisions. Key issues of conflict included issues over the Petrine Docrine (accepted by the West and rejected by the East), issues of celibacy of the priesthood (embraced by the West), and issues on what type of bread was to be used during the Lord's Supper. From this point I will focus the attention on the Western side of the Church.

Another architectural shift took place in the twelfth century to the Gothic form. Gothic was what most define as the cathedral style structure. It featured sharply pointed arches and vaults in doors and windows, balanced thrusts in stone masonry, and steeply pitched gables. This architecture lent itself to extreme heights. The church had moved from a simple, open, and accessible worship space to place filled with multiple chapels and naves, which seemed to reach Heaven itself.

Gothic Cathedral (Pubic Domain Image)

These churches were ornate with their carvings and style. The altar was elaborate and often covered with gold or precious jewels. The walls and spaces were cluttered with images, icons, and frescos. Stained glass moved from color to image-bearing scenes. Music had embedded itself into the liturgy with specific roles for ministers, congregation, choirs, and instrumentalists.

In the Middle Ages (1100-1450 AD), music was a major contributor to the worship service. The organ became a fixture, and music was being written for choir and instrument. Special musical arrangements were composed for the Latin Mass and other special events such as coronations and funerals.

The tragedy in all this was the deepening of the divide between the clergy and laity. The liturgy was remote and was not conducted in the vernacular. The Eucharist was received only by the clergy. In the ignorance of the laity, the words "This is my body. This is my blood" led many to the idea that they were taking part in cannibalism. For all practical purposes, worship was a spectator sport for the laity and a performance by the professional clergy and staff. Dr. Gibbons notes that there was now a distinct tension between what was sacred and what was secular, saying "the liturgy became a sacred action unto itself, a mystery performed for the sanctification of those participating, and, therefore, a displacement of the original meaning." [3]

In the fourteenth century another major change occurred because of the plague called the Black Death. The congregation was not as mobile, and persons would come in all stages of health. Benches or pews began to encroach on the open spaces of the church as the congregation created a place of "being" within the sanctuary. This allowed persons to claim "their space" so they could either separate themselves from the sick or have a better view of the service.

Many additions and traditions had been inserted into the worship liturgy and worship space. Multiple candles, incense, elaborate vestments, prayers for every occasion, all blended together in much pomp and circumstance. Standard liturgical colors were now in place as signs and symbols of the changing church year. These were as follows:

> **White** for Christmas and Easter and their seasons
> **Purple or Violet** for Lent
> **Red** for Holy Spirit, feasts of martyrs, and special occasions such as ordinations
> **Black** for mourning and funerals
> **Green** for Sundays after Pentecost or now called Ordinary Time

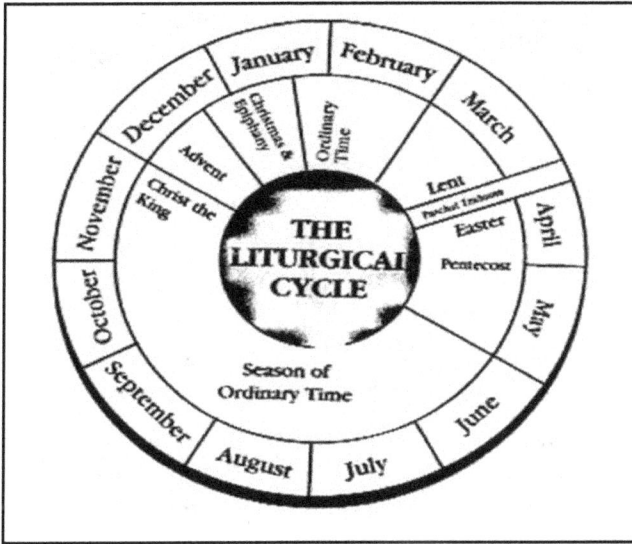

Liturgical Year [4]

Dress for the clergy now carried its own sacredness and with it symbols of rank and holiness. Stoles were added to the attire to establish a distinction between ordained clergy (those set apart for Word and Sacrament) and diaconal ministers (those who performed deeds of service). The Mitre (a stiff cloth hat pointed at the top) and Crosier (a staff curved at the top resembling a shepherd's crook) were symbols of office and authority.

Many say the liturgy of the church was dictated by Constantine, who transported pagan attributes into Christian worship. To some extent, that may be true, but he was simply the catalyst. In reality, the liturgy and worship rubric (the way worship is conducted) found itself adding many of the elements and actions out of need or sacredness. As Frank C. Senn noted, "The history of Christian worship is the story of the give and take between cult and culture." [5] The developed liturgy and worship did not arrive with the church as it came out of hiding. Instead, it developed though years of trial, error, evolution, and moments of passion and sacredness.

Lifting up of the bread and cup. Bringing in the light to begin worship. Carrying out that same light into the world at the end of worship. Incense rising as prayers. Solemnness and sacredness of movement and word brought about by experiencing something holy. These moment-by-moment actions took the simple act of eating around the table with friends and families into the full-blown worship event with all its splendor and holiness.

It was the introduction of the printing press that brought about both unity and conflict. Unity in so much as the church as a whole could not be, as the old saying goes, *singing off the same page*. With mass printing, the material once held privy by the clergy seeped out into the hands of the laity. On differing occasions the laity was reminded that they were only "hearers" of the Word. Clergy were the ones responsible for the reading and interpreting scripture. It makes one wonder, "Why did people even go to church?" Was it out of the need to connect with the community? Was it out of guilt or duty? Was it for the salvitic nature of forgiveness?

The Church worship was now fully developed. The "orders" were critically defined. For all practical purposes, all know their place. But to maintain these elaborate houses of worship and to support the ever-growing number of clergy, the church had to raise additional capital. As the practice of canceling one's sins by giving money to the church, termed indulgences, became popular, the church began to abuse the intention. The struggle of what it really cost to acquire salvation brought the next era of the church into view.

But let us not leave on a negative note. Worship had changed. What was once a simple home gathering had become an elaborate celebration. Let us stop and place ourselves in that space.

As we stand in the nave bathed by a rainbow of light streaming in through stained glass windows, a voice calls out chanting a call to worship. A processional of worship leaders moves towards the front of the cathedral. The crucifer leads the procession with a cross held high, followed by those about to lead in worship. Moving forward, we become aware of the splendor of the magnificent tapestries, paintings, and statues. The altar is adorned with Eucharistic elements and candles as the fragrance of incense fills the air. The priests, shrouded in embroidered chasubles, make their way behind the table. Prayers are said. Music supports the moment. The Gospel is read and proclaimed. The Great Thanksgiving echoes off the stone walls as the mystery is acknowledged. Processing out of the church, we are left standing, pondering the full range of emotion and experience which has just taken place. No, it is not so much about color, smell, sound, and mystery—it is about coming into a sacred space where worshipers connect with the Divine.

Questions for Reflection

1) The Nicene Creed was created as a foundational statement to unify the church. When you say the Nicene Creed or the Apostle's Creed are you aware that what you say is more than a casual statement but the theological boundaries of the church? Does your worship include the affirming of your faith by some creed or statement? Do you think the affirming of your faith is a necessary part of worship?

2) Professional clergy appeared with the establishment of the church "above ground." Those religious leaders wore special vestments or clothing which identified them as clergy. Should the professional clergy continue (or begin) the wearing of clothing which identifies them as such?

3) The early church filled its worship space with collections of paintings, tapestries, icons, and symbols. What symbolism is found in your worship space? Which symbol carries the most significant meaning for you? Why?

4) The church built structures which reflected their approach to worship. When you enter your sanctuary, auditorium, or worship place, what is the central focus of that space?

5) The chapter concludes with the statement: "it is not so much about color, smell, sound, and mystery – it is about coming into a sacred space where one connects with the Divine." Where in your worship space, or during the worship service, do you most connect to God?

Endnotes

[1] Nicene Creed, 381 AD.

[2] Robin Gibbons, House of God: House of the People of God. Ashford Colour Press, Great Britain, 2006. pg 50, 54.

[3] Ibid pg 139.

[4] Liturgical Cycle image granted through http://www.stmaryolg.org/images/liturgicalcycle.gif.

[5] Frank Viola and George Barna, Pagan Christianity? Exploring the Roots of Our Church Practices. BarnaBooks, 2008. pg 78.

Chapter 6

The Deconstruction of Worship
Transitions Brought About By Protestantism

Over the years it seems as if the Church forgot one very special thing—worship was to find oneself in the presence of God. What began as a "spirit filled" lay movement had become a structured worship rubric. This set apart the clergy as those who conducted worship and dictated who could speak, approach the altar, take part in the liturgy and created a "them-us" atmosphere between themselves and the common person. They removed the laity from the worship experience through use of mysterious language, symbols, and actions.

If any one thing provided the catalyst transformation of the Church, it was the 1439 invention by Johannes Gutenberg. Through his new method of movable type, Gutenberg paved the way for moving books from the elite and educated and placing them into the hands of the common people. In the later Middle Ages, this began to empower the laity. They found new religious experiences through their ability to own a personal copy of a prayer book or religious manual. The hymns of the church were being performed in the local vernacular. Suddenly, the common, ordinary, everyday Christian found new freedom in his/her ability to think, pray, and conduct personal worship experiences. The downside of this new resource was that it began turning the laity into Pharisaical finger-pointers. They now could observe others' actions and correct them by pointing to a verse on a page declaring, "See! You can't do that!"

What one may define as a crack in the church vessel

may be better illustrated by a hammer hitting the vessel. At first there is a major crack, then a hole, then the entire vessel crumbles. That "hammer" landed firmly on the church door.

Martin Luther nailing his 95 Theses to the church door
(Public Domain Image)

Martin Luther (1583-1546) was an Augustinian monk, who arrived at Wittenburg University to teach philosophy and while there received his doctorate in Theology. He was a lecturer at the University, teaching the Psalms, Letter to the Romans, Letter to the Galatians, and Letter to the Hebrews. Apparently Luther had already been disturbed by the church's use of indulgences inferring that salvation was to be given and bought through the avenue of church. It is said it was during his lectures on Romans that the theological light came on and he realized that money had nothing to do with salvation. Susan White, lecturer at Cambridge, England, wrote that

> Luther had a very firm conviction that many of the prevailing practices were based on a notion that one's salvation could be earned through good works rather than by coming to God's grace through faith alone.

Masses for the dead, the celibacy of the clergy, the monastic life, pilgrimages, the withholding of the eucharistic wine from the laity, the mediatorial role of the ordained ministry, and the belief that in the eucharist the sacrifice of Christ was repeated ... all fell under Luther's condemnation. [1]

The pressure which built inside the magma of indulgences finally erupted in the sounding of a hammer on the church door. On October 13, 1517, Luther posted his "95 Theses." The actual "nailing of the Theses" has been put under much historical scrutiny. Many say it never happened. However, Luther did send copies to a few bishops and friends. In a short time these made their way to the printing press and were widely circulated. Selected sections of Luther's Theses read as follows:

> Out of love for the truth and from desire to elucidate it, the Reverend Father Martin Luther, Master of Arts and Sacred Theology and ordinary lecturer therein at Wittenberg, intends to defend the following statements and to dispute on them in that place. Therefore he asks that those who cannot be present and dispute with him orally shall do so in their absence by letter. In the name of our Lord Jesus Christ, Amen.
> When our Lord and Master Jesus Christ said, "Repent" (Mt 4:17), he willed the entire life of believers to be one of repentance.
> Those who believe that they can be certain of their salvation because they have indulgence letters will be eternally damned, together with their teachers.
> Any truly repentant Christian has a right to full remission of penalty and guilt, even without indulgence letters.
> Christians are to be taught that he who gives to the poor or lends to the needy does a better deed than he who buys indulgences.

> Injury is done to the Word of God when, in the same sermon, an equal or larger amount of time is devoted to indulgences than to the Word.
> The true treasure of the church is the most holy gospel of the glory and grace of God.
> But this treasure is naturally most odious, for it makes the first to be last (Mt. 20:16).
> Christians should be exhorted to be diligent in following Christ, their Head, through penalties, death and hell.
> And thus be confident of entering into heaven through many tribulations rather than through the false security of peace (Acts 14:22).

Whether or not Luther truly nailed these to the church doors at Wittenburg, the hammer (real or imagined) sounded loud and strong. The sound waves carried to Rome and bounced around the empires. The new-found freedom bound in robes of "Justification by Faith" called persons to stand against the abuses of the Church --to "protest" the old ways. As a result, these rebels were called Protestants. But we know this: before Luther, worship was about the sacrament; after Luther, worship centered around preaching.

Have you ever been driving down the highway when an oncoming vehicle threw up some type of road debris against the windshield? Suddenly you see a hole or chip in the glass. Then, if left unchecked, the chip begins to expand into a spider web of cracks. If the weather turns hot, the glass may finally rupture into a million tiny shards, but to your surprise, the windshield holds together. It is able to do this because of a layer of material between the plates of glass that bonds them together. Over the next eighty years or so, the unified church became much like that shattered glass. So many pieces yet still bound together by unifying strength of Christ. Even among the vast ocean of diversity, the Church was held together by the common understanding of God the

Creator; Jesus the Son, who came to earth, lived out an example for us to follow, was crucified, buried and arose; and the Holy Spirit who continues to reside among those created in the very shadow of the Creator.

Luther was the stone that hit the windshield. In his reformed worship service, the *Formula Missae to Communionis* of 1523, Luther outlined the liturgy of the worship service. Initially the service remained in Latin, but later he became convinced the service should be in the vernacular of the local congregation. He retained many of the Catholic rite rubrics. Luther moved the altar from the wall to the center of the chancel. He brought to a higher place the reading of the scripture, the preaching, the recitating of the Lord's Prayer, and the giving of the communion (Eucharist) elements, both bread and wine, to the laity. Later, Luther composed hymns in German for congregational singing.

Ulrich Zwingly, the leader of the Swiss Reformation, was one who came, quite independently, to the same conclusions as did Luther. Zwingly's battle cry was *sola scriptura*— scripture alone. He later came into possession of Luther's writings, and while Luther led the charge of change in Germany, Zwingly did the same in Switzerland.

On many theological issues Luther and Zwingly agreed, but there were two primary points of conflict. The first had to do with the understanding of the eucharist. Zwingly opposed the notion that the bread and wine became the carnal presence of Christ—that the elements became the physical presence of Christ. Zwingly argued the elements only represented the presence of Christ. And on the issue of baptism, Zwingly held a similar view. Baptism did not "wash away sin" but was only an outward sign of that gift of forgiveness.

During this same time-frame, a group called the Anabaptist arose, rebelling against "the state sanctioned church." Insisting the church should be independent from civil government, their major act of rebellion came in the arena of baptism. They no longer would allow their infants to be baptized but would reserve the act of baptism for those who were old enough to understand and accept the responsibility the act brought. The process for these adults came in the form of often taking a milk pail and pouring the water over the believer's heads, soaking them rather than immersing them. Thus was born the concept of "believer's baptism."

One Anabaptist did not think the church was going far enough from the teachings of Luther and Zwingly. Melchior Hoffman, a leather-dresser, began to mount the pulpit with his "dooms-day" proclamation announcing the "day of the Lord is near." Thus began the apocalyptic preaching better known as a "turn or burn" sermon. Under the influence of Hoffman and Menno Simons, this conservative group was later called Mennonites. From this Annabaptist movement came denominations and groups such as the Quakers, Puritans, Amish, Adventist, and Baptist (General and Peculiar).

In the 1530's John Calvin developed his theology which created the Reformed Churches. One of their primary theological doctrines was that of predestination. Calvin also began the practice of preaching twice on Sundays.

Another major shift came in 1534. Henry VIII, King of England, sought an annulment from a marriage, which was not granted by the Pope. Henry decided that if Rome would not accept his request then he would create a church that would. The Church of England was born and Thomas Cranmer was commissioned to structure the church. *The Book of Common Prayer* was the result of his work. Cranmer changed the approach to the eucharistic elements, stating that nothing happens to the elements, but rather the service of communion was a celebration of the presence of Christ. Another shift from Roman idealism was allowing clergy to marry.

Unlike those who were abandoning structured worship, the Anglican Church found their spirituality based in a scripted style of worship called Liturgical. The church service was based on the Catholic Rite. They did abandon the use of Latin and created an English liturgy for the English-speaking people.

Around 1560, John Knox from Scotland pressed forward the reformation spirit. Known for his powerful preaching, Knox was called "The Thundering Scot." From his preaching and influence came the founding of the Presbyterian Church.

In 1650, there was another division in the Anabaptist movement, led by young cobbler George Fox. He declared that

> If God does not dwell in houses made by human hands, how dare anyone call those buildings where they gather "churches"? They are in truth no more than houses with belfries. ... Hymns, orders of worship, sermons, sacraments, creeds, ministers—they are all human hindrances to the freedom of the Spirit. [2]

Worship did not include any formal structure as they insisted that structure hindered the freedom of the Spirit. Fox named his following "Friends," but because of their unusual worship style, the outside community called them Quakers.

In England, three men began to change the Anglican Church. John Wesley, Charles Wesley, and George Whitefield began systematic examination of not only scripture but also life as well. First called "Bible Moths," the name most often used to describe their dedication was "methodists."

Whitefield was known for his preaching, which often was done out of doors. He created a pattern for what he termed "evangelical preaching." He would base his sermon on a short selected Biblical text and would then move through the process including a short introduction, background information on the text, a listing and exposition on the major points of the text, and a conclusion.

John Wesley, already an Anglican Priest, had his "heart warming" experience after a meeting on Aldersgate Street, May 24, 1738. This changed his perception of how one relates to Christ in a personal way. After preaching a sermon on his experience at St. Mary's Church in Oxford, he was banned from all the pulpits in Oxford. He moved the church out into the streets.

The American Revolution led to another shift. After the war, the many Anglican priests, being British, returned home, leaving multitudes of people without a priest to offer them guidance, support, and, most of all, the sacraments. Wesley took it upon himself to ordain two men, Francis Asbury and Thomas Coke, and sent them to America to begin the work of ministering to the people. This was a frontier church. By necessity it left behind the finery of a liturgical service and moved to a much simpler pattern of worship. On the roads and paths of a new nation, the Methodist Movement came into full view.

This body divided in 1848 over the issue of slavery and the church's failure to embrace the full spirit of the Gospel. Moving for a more conservative doctrine, this group grasped a theology of a two-step plan of salvation—Saved and Sanctified. They took strong stands against secret societies and the wearing of jewelry and abstinence from the use of tobacco and alcohol. Their preaching was spirited and driven on the wings of urgency—Jesus will come back soon. These churches were known as Holiness Churches.

Some thought the Holiness Church did not go far enough in removing their members from the wilds of the world. Adding more energetic music, loud fiery sermons, and speaking in "unknown tongues" as proof of God's Spirit in a believer, the Pentecostal Churches were born.

In the 1870's the freed slaves created a church with Methodist roots, calling themselves the Colored Methodist Episcopal Church or the CME Church. (That name was changed in 1954 to Christian Methodist Episcopal Church.) Their worship was very free and expressive. The songs were based on life's experiences. The sermons were antiphonal as the congregation "helped" the preacher through the service. And, they were not bound by the clock. They finished when they were finished.

With each step along the path of division the theological understanding affected not only how individuals think about their faith but also the space they worship in, the music they embrace, and the way in which worship itself is carried out. These changes were made by charismatic leaders who challenged the people. I will not go into further detail about the communicative skills of those leaders as I have addressed those issues in a previous work *Gospeltelling to a Digital Culture.* [3] However, I will offer the illustration of the growth of the church from that work which offers a visual expansion of the church.

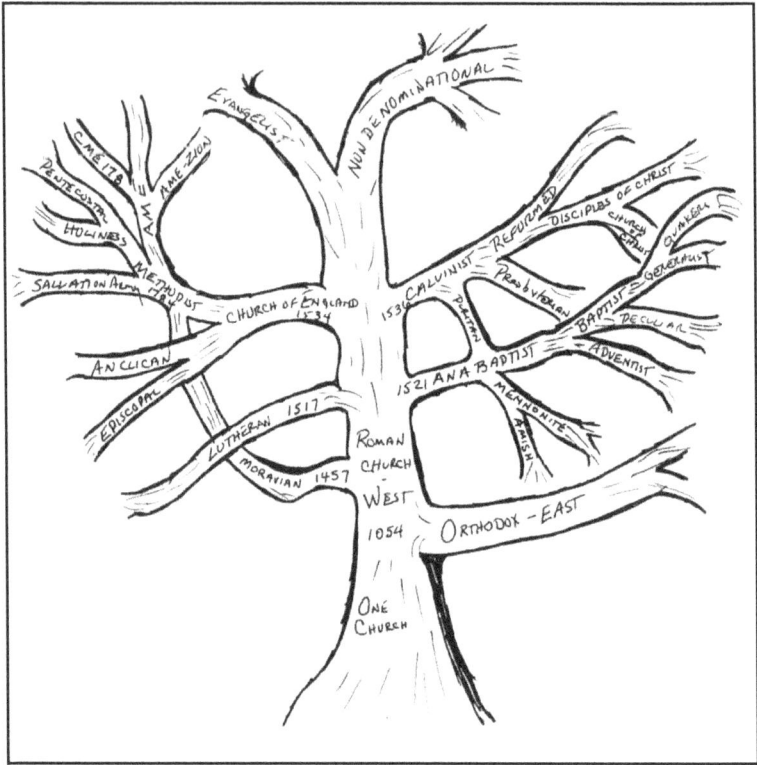

The Spreading Tree of Church Growth (D. Jonathan Watts)

The shift in theology and preaching brought with it a change in purpose and direction of music in the church. Music began as psalms and scriptures put to meter and tune for the purpose of emphasizing the focus of worship. The "ordinary" mass in the Roman Church included at least five different musical selections: the Kyria Eleison, Gloria, Credo, Sanctus, and Agnus Dei.

Luther brought with him a love of music. Not only did he have a very powerful tenor voice, but he also played the flute and lute (a guitar-style instrument). After translating the liturgy into German, he began to write hymns with powerful words and simple tunes. Johann Walther, a skilled musician, assisted Luther in adding harmonies to these simple tunes. Luther also encouraged others to write hymns for use in the worship service. The Classical Composer's website notes the following:

> The first congregational hymn book, "Geystliche Gesangkbuchlein," was already brought out in a mass printing in 1524. This hymn book was commissioned by Luther in fourpart harmony "in order to give the young men something in place of their drinking and fleshly songs." In other words, from now on, the congregation members themselves were to participate musically in the church service; young wouldbe pastors were not accepted for training before they could demonstrate musical competence. [4]

Of all the hymns written by Luther the most prominent is "A Mighty Fortress Is Our God." The first verse of that hymn is

> A mighty fortress is our God, a bulwark never failing;
> Our helper He, amid the flood of mortal ills prevailing;
> For still our ancient foe doth seek to work us woe;
> His craft and power are great, and, armed with cruel hate:
> On Earth is not his equal. (Martin Luther, 1529)

In response to the schism within the church, the Roman Church called a meeting to address not only the issues facing the church theologically but also the church's relationship and responsibility to the laity. The Council of Trent (1545-1563) addressed issues such as liturgy and sacrament. One major change was in the area of music. Not only was there an affirmation of the use of polyphonic singing (singing in parts) but also that music should be written so the worshiper could participate in the singing.

Jumping a hundred years into the future, the story is told of a father and son walking home from worship one Sunday morning. Frustrated at the heartless singing, again the son began to grumble and complain. Tired of listening to the constant complaining, it is said that the father turned to the son and said, "Well, then, young man, why don't you give us something better to sing?" Isaac Watts rose to the challenge by writing his first hymn, which culminated in the writing of over 600 hymns. Given the title of "The Father of English Hymnody," two of his most familiar hymns are "O God, Our Help in Ages Past," a paraphrase of Psalm 90, and "Joy to the World," based on Psalm 98.

One of the most familiar of all hymns was written by a slave merchant named John Newton. After his conversion he penned the words to "Amazing Grace" in 1748. Even though one of the most favored of the verses, the last stanza beginning "When we've been there ten thousand years" was not a part of the original hymn.

In 1865, a London Methodist clergyman decided to move outside the church to minister to the poor and struggling. William Booth intended to create a "church" for these people and established mission stations where people could come and hear him preach. It is said that his fiery sermons and use of vivid images often stirred people to change their lives and, in turn, do their part in fighting "sin." Booth said, "While women weep, as they do now, I'll fight; while little children go hungry, as they do now, I'll fight; while men go to prison, in and out, in and out, as they do now, I'll fight; while there is a poor lost girl upon the streets, while there remains one dark soul without the light of God, I'll fight. I'll fight to the very end!" It was out of this fervent spirit that the "Salvationists" would go into the street and fight for the lost souls. Empowered to do spiritual warfare and established in a militarylike structure, the name of the organization became the Salvation Army. Many have said it was Booth who began using the bar/pub tunes and street song tunes and putting Christian lyrics to those familiar songs.

With these changes also came the shift from the scriptural hymn to hymns that told stories of life struggles. The Negro Spirituals were often adaptations of work songs. Their lyrics were antiphonal as one would sing out and others would repeat the phrase. Songs were of struggles, fears, and freedom from the bondage of this world. "Swing Low, Sweet Chariot" is one of the most familiar:

> Swing low, sweet chariot,
> Comin' for to carry me home;
> Swing low, sweet chariot,
> Comin' for to carry me home.
> I looked over Jordan, And WHAT did I see,
> Comin' for to carry me home,
> A band of angels comin' after me,
> Comin' for to carry me home.
> If you get there before I do,
> Comin' for to carry me home,
> Tell all my friends I'm comin' too,
> Comin' for to carry me home.

Church music continued to follow the pain and struggles of the people often reflecting a new theology of "hang on." Southern Gospel carried with it messages of little log cabins in heaven and the joys of leaving this world for the next.

In the second half of the twentieth century, folk gospel came into use. Songs often created around the campfires and youth gatherings sought a return to a peaceful and a more serene world.

Music found its way into the "traditions" of the church. It was expected that musical instruments provided the call to worship. (Although rather than calling those gathered to a worshipful atmosphere, it usually was something for the congregation to try to talk above.)

Congregational singing was expected, and, if at all possible, the anthem or special music of the day was performed by a choir or soloist. In the evangelical setting, the service closed with a moving song drawing sinners to the place of repentance.

On the wings of theological and musical notation, the structure of church building also changed. The first noticeable change came when the arrangement of the interior changed. Altars were replaced with communion tables designed to hold the eucharistic elements, a large Bible, brass crosses and flowers. Pulpits took center stage as preaching was the central focus of worship. Others divided the chancel into two sections with a pulpit for the preaching of the Word and a lectern for leading worship and reading the scriptures.

By the thirteenth century, pews became a permanent fixture in churches bringing with them exclusion and ownership. Early pews were "leased" to families and were enclosed. Some had compartments where individuals could put hot coals underneath to provide heat. Others went so far as to include kennels for pets brought to church. This led to the "ownership" of pews as persons found their place and claimed it as their own. How often have we heard stories of innocent visitors sitting down for worship only to have the message whispered in their ears that they are sitting in Mr./ Mrs. So-and-So's seat?

The beautiful glass windows shifted from scenes depicting the life of Christ to memorial windows honoring those faithful saints or appreciated donors to the church. And soon to follow, placing a brass plate on anything and everything given to the church in honor or memory of someone became a standard practice.

As the church began to divide and become more local, the buildings and appointments took on the flavor and status of the local congregation. Those in affluent neighborhoods built stone churches with mahogany pulpits and pews. Those less affluent built concrete block buildings with small steeples. Their windows were colored glass, and the pews and pulpit were pine.

The final note on the structure of the church addresses the inclusion of modern ingenuity—lights in the evening. With the incorporation of gas lights and later the economy of electric lights, congregations were able to meet Sunday and Wednesday evenings.

With these changes came the development of traditions. Covering the eucharistic elements with a white cloth originally done to keep flies away; lighting of the candles (originally used to provide a reading light); genuflexing toward the altar, crucifix, or cross; changing the parament and vestment colors (Does white always have to be used on communion Sunday? No.); and placing of the national flag in the sanctuary. These and many other "traditions" bring with them the question "Why do we do it that way?" The response is usually "Because we have always done it that way!" In reality, it has only been done as long as someone remembers. Someone did it once and the people liked it. The next season it was repeated. Before long, it became a tradition. I am not saying that this is a bad thing. Many of the local traditions came into use because initially they provided something special or sacred to those gathered.

As one follows the paths of these developments, it becomes apparent the polarity of worship styles. These styles fall into three categories: Orthodox, Liturgical, and Non-Liturgical. Each tradition has its unique attributes of sacredness.

The Orthodox worship, primarily the Roman Catholic Church for this document, orders worship on a global scale. In 1570, Pope Pius V decided to unify church worship by establishing a standard for all churches to follow. The Missal orders worship as follows:

> ***Introductory Rites***: Entrance, Greeting, Blessing, Penitential Rite, Kyrie, Gloria, Prayer
> ***Liturgy of the Word:*** Biblical Readings, Homily, Creed, Intercessions
> ***Liturgy of the Eucharist:*** Preparation, Eucharistic Prayer; Communion Rite
> ***Concluding Rite:*** Blessing and Dismissal

Orthodox worship is sensory. Bright, vibrant colors on the appointments and those leading worship. The fragrance of incense, wine, and bread. The pageantry of ancient traditions—some which were understood, others simply accepted. And all of this conducted with the understanding that all those of the faith are doing this same liturgy on a given Sabbath.

The Liturgical worship simplifies the Orthodox pattern. Much of the pageantry and mystery is removed. Even though there are patterns and expectations, each church incorporates its own traditions and patterns. Some churches use liturgical vestments while others dismiss such attire. Some have the same feel as an Orthodox service while others do everything in their power to separate themselves from that tradition. A Liturgical pattern is found in the *United Methodist Book of Worship* as follows:

> ***Entrance:*** Gathering, Greeting, Hymn of Praise, Opening Prayer
> ***Proclamation and Response:*** Prayer for Illumination, Scripture Lesson, Psalm (read or sung), Scripture Lesson, Hymn or Song, Gospel Lesson, Sermon, Response to the Word, Concerns and Prayers, Confession and Pardon, The Peace, Offering
> ***Thanksgiving and Communion:*** Taking of Bread and Cup, The Great Thanksgiving, The Lord's Prayer, Breaking of the Bread, Giving of the Bread and Cup
> ***Sending Forth:*** Hymn or Song, Dismissal with Blessing, Going Forth

Under the umbrella of "liturgical" worship, there is a variety of styles and patterns. The one unifying element is the Lectionary—a three-year cycle of Biblical reading. Each Sunday an Old Testament, Epistle, Psalm, and Gospel Lesson are prescribed. As in Orthodox worship, the expectation is not that they do everything the same but rather that on a given day they hear the same scriptural texts.

Then there is the Non-Liturgical Church. These churches do not have a prescribed order of worship. Their order comes from the local tradition. I grew up in a Non-Traditional church, which had an order of worship rather than a liturgy. Worship often followed this pattern:

> ***Musical Prelude***
> ***Opening Prayer***
> ***Two Congregational Hymns***
> ***Pastoral Prayer***
> ***Hymn***
> ***Offering***
> ***Anthem or Special Music***
> ***Sermon***
> ***Invitational Hymn***
> ***Benediction***

These churches follow no lectionary pattern or liturgical calendar. They are not preoccupied with what the seasonal color is or when the first Sunday in Lent arrives. While in the Liturgical Church communion is served on a regular basis either of every Sunday or at least once a month, these churches may serve the eucharist once a quarter or even once a year. They pride themselves in constructing worship around the moving of the Spirit.

Concluding this chapter, a *deja vu* moment is experienced. Over a period from Constantine to the present, the Church has once again deconstructed itself into a menagerie of styles, liturgies, traditions, and theologies, which were experienced when the church emerged from underground.

Questions for Reflection

1) Where is your faith community located on the Spreading Tree of the Church?

2) Can you name the founders of your denomination or church and their theological beliefs?

3) What are the theological and liturgical elements which separate your denomination from other denominations?

4) Music found itself at the core of Protestant worship. How would you describe the musical genre of your faith community?

5) Describe the order of worship or liturgy of the worship service you prefer.

Endnotes

[1] Paul F. Bradshaw and Lawrence A. Hoffman, ed. The Making of Jewish and Christian Worship. University of Notre Dame Press, Indiana, 1991. pg 185-186.

[2] Justo L. Gonzalez, The Story of Christianity Volume 2:

.

,

Chapter 7

The Battle Lines Are Drawn
The Re-Reformation of the Church

It would be a nice dream that as the church progressed through its metamorphosis each of the new communities went its separate way, being honored and respected for its individual views and preferences. Nothing could be further from the truth. But then again, that should not surprise us. Paul faced the same battles with the scattered faithful of his day. The author of Revelation selected seven churches as examples of the entire community, and no two were alike.

Being a child of the Boomer Generation, I experienced at an early age the tensions between the denominations. The Holiness/Pentecostal churches pointed fingers at the Mainline churches saying they were too liberal. The Mainline churches struggled to be true to a liturgical tradition without appearing "too Catholic." The Roman Catholic church looked at the Protestant churches as one looks at a lost puppy, hoping it finds its way home.

It became a "them vs. us" atmosphere. I remember preachers proclaiming the Pope was the Antichrist and the Catholic Church was the Beast of Revelation. I experienced the heavy-handed, turn-or-burn, Hell-fire sermon which made God appear to be full of revenge and to find joy in casting souls into the sulfur flames of Hades. I envied those who sought to "be like Christ" through simply doing good and helping those in need—doing their best to ignore the flaming arrows of the criticizers. Dogmas were so entrenched that no one trusted or believed anyone else.

This entrenching of the church reminded me of the cartoon *Non Sequitur* which depicted a man and woman passing a church. The doors were heavy-hinged and a bulldog sat guarding the entrance. The sign read "The Church of WE'RE ABSOLUTELY RIGHT and EVERYONE ELSE IS WRONG." [1]

The Boomer Generation began to break the mold of society—both in the secular world and in the church world as well. They no longer accepted the words of their parents, teachers, and ministers as fact. Their battle cry became "Prove it!" And between the emerging drug culture and the tension of a polarizing war, separatists moved away from anything institutional.

The late 1960's were tumultuous times. The Vietnam war was dragging on and many began to protest by burning draft cards and flags. The space program, America's "star in the crown," suffered the tragic Apollo 1 fire on the launch pad, killing three astronauts. Race relations were at a high tension in the wake of the Watts Riots in Los Angeles, California. Blended into all this was a new culture called hippies.

In 1967 a small movement began in a store-front mission in San Francisco. The group was known as *The Jesus Movement*. These brave souls waded out into the treacherous cultural waters of the hippies to bring them a sense of hope and peace. Suddenly this "Prove it" generation embraced Jesus and began to retool the culture. It became "cool" to declare "Jesus is just all right with me!"

These newborns in the faith worshiped in parks and on beaches. Ocean baptisms were common. The call of the preacher/evangelist sounded much like Jonathan Edwards from the Great Awakening years. Fueled by the writing of Hal Lindsey in *The Late Great Planet Earth*, they proclaimed a message that Christ would be returning soon and they could prove it through historical events. The primary event was the independence of Israel.

Music was its most powerful ally. In the spring of 1972, I attended an Ichthus Festival near Asbury Theological Seminary in Wilmore, Kentucky. Dressed in our button-fly jeans with "One Way Jesus" patches, a group from my college gathered at the Woodstock-styled event. I remember how the musicians used current rock-and-roll songs and changed the words. The most memorable was Don McLean's *Starry, Starry Night*. The original lyrics were about Vincent Van Gogh, but this group rewrote the lyrics to be a song about the sacrifice of Jesus.

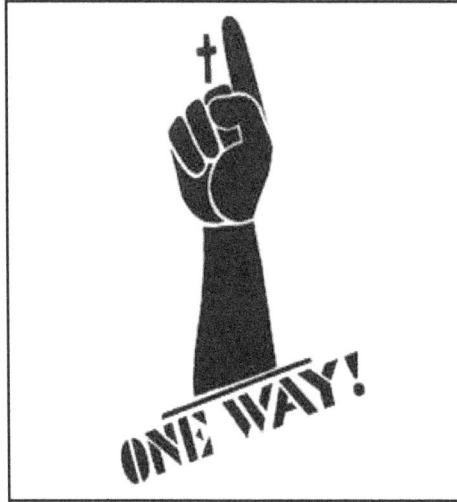

One Way Image used during the Jesus Movement
(and a patch I wore on my jeans) [2]

At college I sang in a musical titled *Natural High* by Ralph Carmichael and Kurt Kaiser. It was written in the language and tenor of the drug culture. The lyrics offered an alternative, stating that a relationship with Jesus was better than drugs. The theme song declared

It's a scientific formula effectively reduced to simple
terms so everyone can try.
It's a perfectly legal, nonchemically induced,
logically natural high.[3]

This brought about a new genre of music, labeled
Contemporary Christian Music. At first, it was music to be
used "outside" the church at festivals and beach gatherings.
Eventually, this music made its way into the youth halls and
finally into the sanctuary of the church. Many of these songs
now reside in the hymnals parked in the pew rack.

Also at this same time the American Bible Society
released its translation of the New Testament scriptures titled
Good News for Modern Man. This translation attempted to
bring the Gospel message down to the understanding level of a
child. Many scholars attacked the effort, saying the volume
"dumbed down" the message. This move basically mirrored
the events of the Reformation, which took foreign/strange
texts and placed them in a language the people could
understand. The most memorable part of the Good News
Bible for me was the stick figure drawings which illustrated
many significant events. Illustrated by Annie Vallotton, the
pictures are simple yet allow the readers to use their
imaginations to fill in the faces, colors and backgrounds.

So the church found itself in a new style of
reformation—an anti-establishment style of worship. The
name "Contemporary Worship" seems so strange to me. Any
worship conducted in the current context is "contemporary."
Luther's worship was "contemporary worship" in 1540. So
was the Quaker, the Methodist, and the Church of Christ
worship. Yet this style began differently. It found itself
starting as a fringe movement, which caused more than a stir.
It captured the imagination of a searching generation. Bill
Hybels, pastor of Willow Creek Community Church, in an

interview with Peter Jennings for a documentary, said that "In The Name Of God" spoke of their desire to reach a new generation. Teams went door-to-door asking first, "Do you go to church?" If the person said "No," the next question was "Why?" He said the most frequent responses were that they did not like old-fashioned music nor did they like old-fashioned sermons.

The movement began in coffee houses and later moved to store-front buildings. These communities did not look like churches. The people were not "dressed" for church. They used loud drums and guitars and sang unfamiliar songs. The churches grew by leaps and bounds in a time when traditional churches were losing members in record numbers. I will not attempt to address all the issues and venues associated with "contemporary" worship since volumes have been written on the how's, when's, and why's of the experience. In my opinion, at least five major shifts have occurred in this new worship phenomenon - music, drama, use of technology, the patterns for preaching/proclamation, and theological trends. Please note these are not criticisms—they are observations. They are my observations born out of my experience of worship.

The first is music. In the beginning worshipers borrowed an old trick from ages past—they used tunes they knew and inserted new words. I remember singing "Amazing Grace" to the tune of "Peaceful, Easy Feeling." Some took old hymns, made the words contemporary (taking out the thees and thous), and changed the meter to be more "up tempo." Often they would take a hymn written in 4/4 time and modify it to 3/4 or swing. As this branch of the church matured, they began writing their own music. Many churches have "praise teams" which not only select the music but also often times write their own for certain occasions.

My observations on this new-style worship music are two-fold. First, in every service I have attended in the "contemporary" style, the expectation is that the congregation stand, clap, and even wave while the musicians lead with praise songs. The problem often arises that the congregation or those gathered do not know the songs or the songs are more "solo" in style. Thus the congregation takes the position of spectators—much like those gathered at a sporting event cheering their team. Music becomes part of the experience—even if that experience is not participating in the proclaiming of the music.

One change in the music venue is its purpose. The "old" hymns, for lack of a better term, were written either to proclaim a Biblical text or to tell a story. That being the case, if one does not sing all the verses of a hymn, part of the story is missing–which is often the case. There is the old tongue-and-cheek saying, "The loneliest thing in the world is the third verse of a hymn." The genre of this music is narrative, while the genre of contemporary worship music is much more inclined to be affirmational. Songs make bold statements and repeat those statements over and over again. Many times there is no definitive end to the song—the musicians take their leads from the Spirit and decide to close the song when they feel "led" to draw it to a close.

A story was once told concerning the differences in music styles. An old country farmer went to the "big city" and while there attended a church with a contemporary worship service. His wife asked him about the differences in how they worshiped:

"Well," he said, "they sing things differently."

"How so?" she asked.

Trying to create a point of reference for his wife he replied, "At our church we would sing 'The brown cow eats green grass. Amen.' But in this contemporary service they would sing, 'The cow, the cow, the brown, brown cow. Eats grass, grass, grass. The brown, brown cow eats grass. Amen.'"

One marvelous benefit to this music is that it is a part of the culture. That being said, many are able to play the instruments to perform the music. Many churches have multiple music teams which rotate from Sunday to Sunday. So, instead of the music being conducted by a selected musical group backed by a single person on an organ or piano, many are able to use their talents in worship and praise. Another observation I have made, after visiting a number of contemporary services, is that many of these are Boomer Generation participants. Those playing keyboard or guitar or drums are post-50 individuals who love rock-and-roll and love to make music.

A by-product of this is the phenomenal grow of music outside the church. One of the fastest growing musical genres is Contemporary Christian music. Since the emergence of Christian radio stations, both commercial and satellite, many songs heard on the air are brought into the church and converted into worship songs.

Another aspect of this style of worship is the incorporation of drama. This is not something new but something reclaimed. Drama became a way of presenting the gospel in the Middle Ages. Some say the rise of Christian drama came into being as a result of such poor preaching. (Maybe that is also the reason for its renewal.) The Passion Play and the Christmas Story were the focus of the early events. Miracle Plays, whose base came from the miracle stories in the Bible, came into vogue during the 12th century. The 15th century ushered in the Morality Play in an attempt to awaken humanity to the judgmental side of the faith.

Today we continue to use drama as part of our worship experience. In the traditional church one finds that almost every church has a Christmas pageant. I remember as a child doing small skits in Vacation Bible School to illustrate the story of the day. The contemporary church has rediscovered the use of drama as a part of the worship. Short skits and dramas are used as a reflection of the theme or text of the day. The resources for plays, skits, and short dramas are numerous. Drama is used to convey the message of the gospel story and the application of that story to our lives today.

The worship space has also undergone a tremendous shift. I remember the days when a church moved into the technological age by purchasing microphones and an amplifier. They took great care to hide every wire and speaker so the congregation would not see the inclusion of new technology. Today wires and speakers hang from ceilings and run across floors with a "who cares" approach. Many of these churches are found in buildings without windows. That being the case, PowerPoint slides and images are now the new stained-glass window of the church. With that technology there is no reason to have hymnals or even Bibles since words and texts are projected on large screens.

The chancel area is now a stage. When the drama is being performed or the pastor begins a sermon, house lights go down and spot lights come on. No longer is the focus on a cross, a pulpit, or a font. The focus is moving and changing with each shift in the service.

In the interview with Bill Hybels, Peter Jennings also addressed the absence of images and icons present in other churches. He boldly said that the reason they do not have a cross on the wall, a bible present before the people, or even a baptismal font on the chancel is that these are things which may "intimidate" people who come to church for the first time. And he is not alone. The pastor of the Ginghamsburg Church in Tipp City, Ohio, a church with an attendance in the thousands each Sunday, not only vacates the space of image but also their "prelude" music is often secular so as not to offend the newcomer.

In this high-tech worship, nothing is fixed. Everything on the stage and on the floor is movable. Some may go so far as to have theater seating, but for the most part one finds individual chairs which can afford the space a variation of look and experience. The "place" of gathering is no longer a "sanctuary" but a worship space/place.

Proclamation of the Word has also undergone change. To leave behind the pattern and process of the liturgical calendar with its fixed texts and readings is nothing new. And even the concept of "thematic" sermons has been in use within many traditions for decades. The new trend put in place is two-fold. First, those proclaiming the Gospel have tended to become more social conscious. Sermons center around relationships, finances, fears, and expectations. One of the loudest complaints from the "old school" theologians is that the new style seems to be more self-help centered than Christ-centered.

The second part of that is instead of using the seasons of the church year, they now produce sermon series, grouped sermons based on a common theme or concept. The hope of the multi-part series is that if the series starts on a good note, no one will want to miss the next part. It would be nice if these preachers were creative enough to develop this material, and some are, but many rely on preaching aids and help to offer guidance and outlines.

Before we begin to cry "foul," I offer assurance that I indeed know the toil and struggles of sermon preparation.

This is not a criticism of a system that seems to bring multitudes into the arms of the church. It is a new world. People live in times when they need direction and guidance. What better place to provide that direction and guidance than the church?

Finally, there is the issue of theology. What does one do with the traditions which have anchored the Church for two thousand years? While studying at Oxford University, Oxford, England, I attended Christ Church College (the college the Wesley boys attended and were ordained). Directly across the street from the entrance to Christ Church is St. Aldates Church, one of the oldest and most famous of the Oxford Churches. The church had been vacated. A group purchased the church and spent an enormous amount of money renovating and upgrading the building. The result was a very non-traditional church. While having lunch one day, I overheard a conversation between two Anglican priests. They were complaining about St. Aldates: "I can't believe the things they do over there! Why they serve the eucharist and then just leave the elements sitting on the edge of the chancel—uncovered!"

I have spoken to pastors of these free-standing, community churches. When I ask them about their theological foundation, the answer is surprising. "We don't have a theology!" one declared. To which I responded, "You do. You just have not acknowledged it." What I have found is that many of these churches are dressed in disguise. They may use the name "community" or "non-denominational" as a title, but many spring from the established roots of the Church and cloak their theology in contemporary terms. I find it interesting that many of the contemporary churches birthed from an established denomination acknowledge that connection in the small print at the bottom of a sign or website—"Big Springs Church" will be in large, bold print, and below, in small, thin type "A United Methodist Congregation" or, as one in my community states, "A Non-Traditional Southern Baptist Church."

My greatest concern in this new tradition is the popcorn effect of new churches. With the only requirement of a space (often being vacant retail or commercial space) and some rather inexpensive technology, anyone can say, "Hey! Let's start a church!" And with nothing more than a heart full of Jesus and a Bible, they begin to preach—void of theological or Biblical training. And when things do not go well, what happens to the gathered? If the pastor leaves or finds him/herself in difficulty, where will the congregation find a new pastor?

In the first Reformation the churches separated and each went their own way. This time the Church had a better plan. Seeing not only the success in attendance but also in their filling a spiritual void in an absent generation, churches decided to claim the old adage: If you can't beat them—join them. And so the mainline churches opened up their fellowship halls and gyms and embraced this new worship style. They offered these services at alternative times—early in the morning, Saturday evening. Some even dared to set them side-by-side with the traditional style of worship.

Soon one could hear the low rumbles in the churches grumbles and mumbles about how "those" people are not doing worship in the right way. How their music is too loud. How their singing and hand waving is too emotional. How they should know better than to come to church dressed like that! And now the church is divided—we do not know each other. Suddenly the battle lines are drawn.

I do not sense this tension between the free-standing contemporary churches and traditional churches. However, I find a great deal of tension where mainline churches have moved to offer both styles of worship.

In an article written by Mary E. Biedron, titled "Traditional/Contemporary: What Matters To You?" Rev. Biedron notes, "At times it seems as though people are genuinely 'taking sides' on the issue of contemporary vs. traditional worship."[4] And she raises some very specific arguments heard in the ranks of the traditional church. Her questions include the following:

1) Are we creating separate congregations?
2) Are we discarding the past?
3) Are we helping people to participate and take leadership in worship?
4) Is there theological depth?
5) Are we allowing time for contemplation and stillness?
6) Are we worshiping as God has called and led us? [5]

Melody Pugh in an article written for *Christianity Today International* states:

The embattled contemporary worship scene has faced charges of being trite, of sacrificing quality for popularity. It's been accused of self-centeredness and too narrow an understanding of what and who benefits from worship. But we shouldn't ignore the fact that contemporary worship carries strong overtones of God's acceptance of the praise of all his people, rich or poor, sophisticated or simple. It offers opportunity to use the gifts of a greater number of people, acknowledges differing cultural traditions, and often biblically meets the culture on it own territory. [6]

The tensions once reserved for factions of the church as they pointed fingers and accused each other of not worshiping in the "right way" have now turned inward. Lines have been drawn within the halls and hallowed places. Those traditionalists claim that the contemporary have abandoned all that is right and holy for the sake of production and flare. The contemporary accuse the traditionalists of being boring, flat, and out of touch with the current generation.

One of the most familiar complaints from the traditional side of the line is contemporary worship has discarded all tradition. Well, who has defined "tradition?" Are traditional elements those concepts born out of Scripture? Are they the elements handed down over two thousand years? Or are they traditions of a local church started by Aunt Sally fifty years ago and, to keep peace in the congregation, still continue today?

The rebuttal to that argument often comes from those within the contemporary movement who declare they are only getting back to the "original" church patterns. What they seek is a place where they can find simple structure, few rules, and fellowship-centered worship.

In a conversation I had with a founder of a "community church," he stated they were a 1 Timothy church. In 1 Timothy 3, the author offers patterns for the early church as seen in these excerpts:

1 Timothy 2:

[8]I want everyone everywhere to lift innocent hands toward heaven and pray, without being angry or arguing with each other. [9]I would like for women to wear modest and sensible clothes. They should not have fancy hairdos, or wear expensive clothes, or put on jewelry made of gold or pearls. [10]Women who claim to love God should do helpful things for others, [11]and they should learn by being quiet and paying attention. [12]They should be silent and not be allowed to teach or to tell men what to do.

1 Timothy 3

It is true that anyone who desires to be a church official wants to be something worthwhile. ²That's why officials must have a good reputation and be faithful in marriage. They must be selfcontrolled, sensible, wellbehaved, friendly to strangers, and able to teach. ³They must not be heavy drinkers or troublemakers. Instead, they must be kind and gentle and not love money. .... ⁸Church officers should be serious. ... ⁹And they must have a clear conscience and hold firmly to what God has shown us about our faith.   ¹⁰They must first prove themselves. Then if no one has anything against them, they can serve as officers.¹¹Women must also be serious. They must not gossip or be heavy drinkers, and they must be faithful in everything they do. ¹²Church officers must be faithful in marriage. They must be in full control of their children and everyone else in their home.¹³Those who serve well as officers will earn a good reputation and will be highly respected for their faith in Christ Jesus.¹⁴I hope to visit you soon. But I am writing these instructions, ¹⁵so that if I am delayed, you will know how everyone who belongs to God's family ought to behave. After all, the church of the living God is the strong foundation of truth. (1 Timothy 2 and 3 CEV)

I understand the text in relation to a culture of two thousand years ago which was strongly patriarchal. That being the case, I smile every time I think of the statement about being a 1 Timothy church. I smile because I have attended that church, and, if nothing else, these twenty-first century women are not holding true to the first-century edicts. But I understand the concept: Get back to the basics. Do all in the name of Christ and for the sake of the Kingdom.

Whether they want to accept the fact or not, the Contemporary Church is creating its own tradition. The music its worshipers use, the way they dress, the pattern of worship eventually becomes embedded in the fabric of the church, and when *that* occurs, then *that* becomes tradition.

No matter what church a person attends, what denomination a person attaches to, whichever style of worship a person prefers, it always creates traditions—and traditions are made by those epiphany moments in the life of a church when those gathered recognize a theophany moment—a God appearance in their midst. They do everything in their power to relive that event over and over again—and that becomes tradition.

I think the Reverend John Dreyer said it well: "I believe these terms 'traditional' and 'contemporary' are unclear terms and divisive to the church. When I studied philosophy, I learned a fundamental principle: 'Everything is a matter of definition.' When the 'definition' is unclear, so is the conversation." [7]

And that is what brought me to this challenging event of writing. I spoke in the introduction about the Sunday School class which struggled over what they termed worship. When I innocently stepped into the waters of worship, I suddenly found myself in the midst of a raging flood and violent storm of voices thundering about "right' worship. They complained about "those" who have taken "right" worship and watered it down, jazzed it up, and removed its spirituality. These are people who had grown into their faith in the confines of what is often termed "traditional" worship. Not all were down on the contemporary style. Coming to the defense of friends and family, they were quick to add that if that was what they liked, then let them have it.

Well, what is the "it"? Who has the right to define
"it"? Who has the authority to own "it?" In an interview
James Carville quoted Mark Shields as saying, "Do you want
to be in a church that's chasing out heretics, or do you want to
be in a church that is bringing in converts?" And is that not
the point of it all? In a place where we have drawn a battle
line of right way versus other way, is it not all about bringing
others to that place of meeting Jesus? Just as the Reformation
opened the doors of the church to those who had never heard
the message of Christ, so is the Re-Reformation. For those
who would never enter the doors of a steepled church, they
will enter the glass doors of a store-front building or the side
door leading to a fellowship hall.

Let us journey through a Re-Reformation worship
service. We enter the dimly lighted worship space. Music is
playing, and announcements and scriptures are being flashed
on the multiple projection screens. Suddenly the images
disappear to a screen which begins a numerical count-down to
worship. The lights go up; the music is energetic. The
gathered rise to their feet as they join the praise team leaders
in praise songs. Some sing loudly. Some simply rock back
and forth. Others lift their hands. There is a time of welcome,
instruction, and offering. A drama team displays their talents,
acting out a scene describing the issue or topic to be addressed
later. The praise team sings a song they have written just for
this moment of worship. The pastor moves to the center of the
stage as the house lights go dark, and there the spot-light
becomes for him or her the vestment for proclamation. As we
come to the close of the service, a song brings it all together—
and I do mean all together.

> When the music fades. All is stripped away. And I
> simply come, longing just to bring something that's of
> worth that will bless Your heart I'll bring You more
> than a song. For a song in itself is not what You have
> required. You search much deeper within. Through the

> way things appear.
> You're looking into my heart
> I'm coming back to the heart of worship.
> And it's all about You, It's all about You, Jesus.
> I'm sorry, Lord, for the thing I've made it
> When it's all about You, It's all about You, Jesus. [8]

And in all our struggles is that not the basis of every new community of faith over the centuries? Trying our best, from who we are, to make worship ALL ABOUT JESUS?

Even with that unifying thought, there are still those drawing lines in the sand, making claims to battle against those who do not do it right. Can we not simply find a place of truce and find within ourselves the ability to trust? As Gamaliel told the gathered Sanhedrin concerning the new sect springing from the Jewish community, "I tell you, keep away from these men and let them alone; because if this plan or undertaking is of human origin, it will fail; but if it is of God, you will not be able to overthrow them—in that case you may even be found fighting against God!" (Acts 5: 38-39 NRSV)

Questions for Reflection

1) When you discuss "Christian denominations," do you find yourself placing groups in categories of "us" and "them"? What separates your faith community from other faith communities?

2) Some denominations prefer a particular translation of the Bible. Which translation does your church use during its worship? Which translation do you prefer for your personal devotional time?

3) There are three primary styles of worship at work within the Protestant church: traditional, contemporary, and blended. Which style of worship do you prefer? Why?

4) Most churches now use technologies to enhance their worship such as PowerPoint, video, and sound amplification. What technologies are in use during your worship service?

5) If you sense tensions within your own worship community over the differing styles of worship, describe the elements which seem to create that tension?

Endnotes

[1] Wiley Miller, Non Sequitur, 03/15/2009.

[2] Image used with permission.

[3] Ralph Carmichael and Kurt Kaiser, *Natural High: A Folk Musical About God's Son,* 1970

[4] Mary E. Biedron, *Traditional/Contemporary: What Matters to You?* North Congregational Church, Farmington Hills, Michigan. Article undated.

[5] Ibid

[6] Melody Pugh, *Worship Wars: Whose Songs Exalt God More?* Christianity Today Library.
        http://www.ctlibrary.com/newsletter/ newsletterarchives/20060307.html

[7] Rev. John Dreyer, *Contemporary vs Traditional: What Do We Really Mean.* Concordia Theological Seminary, Fort Wayne, Indiana. Article undated.

[8] Matt Redman. "The Heart of Worship."

Chapter 8

A View from the Edge of a Cloud
We all look the same from here – so how do we erase the Battle Line?

I have a cartoon taped to my office door — just in case someone comes by to talk about religion. It is another from the comic Non Sequitur. (For those who do not know, a wealth of Biblical and theological information can be found in the funny-papers.) The scene is of a large entrance nestled in the clouds. The arching sign overhead says "Welcome to Heaven." Two gates, separated by a small wall with two signs, allow entrance into Heaven. One sign reads "Right Religion Entrance" pointing to the gateway on the right. The other sign says "Wrong Religion Entrance" and points to the left. A mass of people are passing through the right gate. The left gate has no one. Two angels are standing over to one side viewing the processional. One smiles and says, "The funny thing is none of them ever get the joke."[1] On the Battle Fields of Worship, both sides hold up the banner "Right Worship." This speaks of an approach too often taken by the church. We speak in terms of "them" and "us," "liberal" and "conservative," "Right Worship" and "Wrong Worship."

Early in my ministerial career, I was a member of a liturgical order. I studied the liturgy and rubric of the worship. I rehearsed how to hold the bread and cup during the eucharistic liturgy. I researched the proper model for baptism. I studied the order of worship to properly place the reading of the Letter and the Gospel. I lived with the question "Am I sure I am doing it right?" I made the art of liturgy a part of my discipline. I incorporated them into my worship-being. Later, I realized not everyone wanted or needed to worship in the ancient way.

I have been challenged by those in my congregation asking why we have to say the Apostles's Creed and Lord's Prayer every Sunday. And I have been affirmed by one who shared with me that he did not like the "order" of worship when he first began to attend the church and how he now finds a sense of spiritual comfort in the creed and prayer. I have faced down those who wanted to change the creed to read "Universal" not "Holy Catholic" church because that sounded—well—too Catholic. And I have had those who listened to the purpose of the words admit they did not understand but now embrace being a part of the entirety of God's church.

I see no reason that everyone who marches under the banner of Christian be required to go back to the "original" way of worshiping—if anyone can actually define the concept of "original." Worshipers need only to go as far enough back in tradition to reach a place which creates for them a sense of holiness. We do not come to worship because "we" have made the place holy but because the presence of God among us made it that place holy.

I cannot come this far without some sense of resolve. What can we do to relieve the tension between the worship communities—especially when they find themselves under one roof? And this is where I have experienced the most tension. The members of a "free standing" contemporary church often respond saying "you do your thing—I'll do mine." But in-house, where upstairs the "traditional" people gather and downstairs the "contemporary" folk congregate, it is a different matter. It was in the midst of this tension where the discussion began to provide seed for this work. And this is not an isolated occurrence. I find that in other churches in other communities the same tense voice is heard. It came down to a *them* and *us* territorial battle. So from the depth of my soul I ask: "For the sake of Christ and His Church, can't we just get along?"

Much tension arises not because of our correctness or Biblical foundation but from purely personal expectation. In the summer of 1993, I was attempting to finish my Doctor of Ministry document. The church I served supported me in this effort and "gave" me the month of August to complete the work. During this time all that was expected of me was to take care of the needy and preach on Sunday mornings. On a trip up to my wife's home, her mother asked:

> "So, what are you doing on Wednesday night this summer?"
>
> I replied, "I am not doing anything on Wednesday night."
>
> "What!! You are not having church on Wednesday night?" she declared.
>
> "No. Jesus never went to church on Wednesday night."
>
> After a long pause she then asked, "Well, what are you doing on Sunday night?"
>
> "Nothing. Jesus did not go to Sunday night church either," I said.

The point was if we want to go back, then we must go all the way back. To do worship the "right" way, as some define, one must also remember Jesus was not a Christian; he was Jewish—and from what I read a very devout Jew.

And it is with that thought I will dare to make some very bold statements. Jesus did not come to establish the church. He came to make disciples who would gather as the church. The Great Commission was not to go out and build the church or even make the world "Christian." It was to make disciples. In an email, Leonard Sweet wrote to reminded me that the first two letters in the word God are g and o. Jesus never tried to prepare us for the after-life. He tried to prepare us to be better people in this life. To accomplish that, we must gather to learn the art of being Christian.

In a similar theme, the church spent 1500 years shifting from being a place of "spirit" to a place of "sacredness and sacrament." Since the Reformation the community has tried its best to go back to the place of the spirit. We have moved from The Light to a house full of candles. We have shifted from gathering around the Table to waiting for an invitation even to approach the table. When will we realize it is not about what we give to God but how we receive God? The church has experienced a paradigm shift from a place of faith and worship to a place of deliverance and rescue—from salvation to self-help. The church was never meant to be a "salvation station." It was to be a place to refuel the soul, so the worshiper could go out and live a life that attracts others to Christ. George Barna said, "Are we living in a culture that is so infiltrated with change that we have forgotten that the church is about transformation, not mere change?" [2]

In trying to reach a place of understanding, the reason behind the conflict, I developed a survey. I distributed the questions on paper and also asked the same questions to those in other communities. The survey began by listing definitions of music, preaching, order of worship, the worship space, and attire. On the form I asked for a response to these two questions:

1) What worship style do you prefer?

I prefer a traditional style of worship
I prefer a contemporary style of worship
I prefer a blended style of worship

2) What things do you like about that worship style?

In your worship experience, list the three most important elements of worship:

The results were interesting. Of those surveyed, 58% preferred traditional style worship. In each of the three worship styles, the two most preferred elements of worship were music and preaching/sermon. Those who selected the "blended" style, by definition and answer, were more closely related to the contemporary style worship, so I combined their responses. Here are the statistics:

For those who selected Traditional Style of Worship - The most important elements:

Music	96%
Sermon/Preaching	89%
Prayer	32%
Order of Worship	21%

For those who selected Contemporary/Blended Worship - The most important elements:

Music	80%
Preaching	65%
Prayer	38%
Casual Dress	38%

As with any survey, I had some preconceived ideas as to the outcome. What surprised me is that whichever style of worship that is desired, the top three most important features of worship are the same—music, preaching, and prayer.

Music from the very beginning of humankind has been a conduit to the holy. From Jubal, the ancestor of musicians (Genesis 4:21), to David playing his harp and singing psalms, from the disciples joining voices in the upper room to the powerful productions of Mozart and Bach, from hymns of Isaac Watts to the praise music of Andrae Crouch—each generation has found that music lifts the soul heavenward. During my years of parish ministry, I often said, "Good music will carry a bad sermon a long way." The survey results tell me that it does not matter the style of music one prefers; it is that the music connects with the soul. That is primary among those who gather for worship.

The second element of worship is the preaching/ proclamation of the Word. Here many of the respondents placed footnotes concerning their preference. They used terms such as "Bible-based sermons" or "scriptural" sermons. They wanted the sermon to be meaningful and well prepared. They desired to leave the place of worship with something to carry home. During my days of preaching each week, my wife informed me that if I did not teach/tell her something new then she should not bother to come and listen.

I know there are differences in preaching styles. Those in traditional worship desire a more exegetical sermon which takes a text and expands it into today's world. Those in contemporary worship desire more thematic sermons but still want those points of learning and direction to be Biblically-based. The desire of all was good, theologically sound, Biblically accurate sermons.

The third important element of worship is prayer. Prayer also comes in a menagerie of approaches. Some services have written prayers with responses. Some churches have spontaneous prayers offered up by persons standing or kneeling at their pews. Some churches pray using the solo voice of the preacher or liturgist while others use a corporate model as all lift their voices together. However produced, the people expect a place in the worship service where they stop to look boldly into the face of God and say, "Lord, here I am again."

These three elements of worship are the common ground. Here lies the place of truce where we say, "I believe that too." Now we have only to leave the judgment of rightness up to God and simply trust each other enough to say, "I hope you encountered God today." It is within this statement the Battle Lines of Worship are erased.

Worship morphs into the shape of the spiritual needs of the community. In these fast-changing times, there will come a day when others will say "That style does not meet my need" and will create a new worship experience. When they do, there will be those pointing their fingers declaring, "That is not the way you are supposed to do it!"

When I pass that cartoon on my door, I often get that sinking feeling that the concept is all wrong. It is not a place of "right" or "wrong." From what I find in the scriptures, there is nothing telling me that on one corner in Heaven a person will find a First Methodist Church and on another First Baptist Church and in the center a Catholic Cathedral. What I sense is a place where all God's children come together at that place of truce and trust and enter through a common door. If I were a part of that cartoon, I would step over to the edge of the cloud where I could look down on the world and all its troubles. I see within this sea of turmoil a place of hope nestled within the gathered congregations. From up here, we all look the same.

Questions for Reflection

1) In the survey of worship priorities, the first three primary desires of the worship communities were music, preaching, and prayer. Name some other important elements of a worship service.

2) List your "top three" most important elements of worship.

3) After traveling this journey, what has changed in your perception of worship and what has remained the same?

Endnotes

[1] Wiley Miller, <u>Non Sequitur</u>, 10/29/2009.

[2] Voila/Barna, pg xxvi.

ABOUT THE AUTHOR

D. Jonathan Watts, Ph.D., teaches Religion and Ethics at Snead State Community College, Boaz, Alabama and is the John Wesley Professor of Homiletics and Biblical Studies for the Graduate Theological Foundation, South Bend, Indiana. He is an ordained Elder in the North Alabama Conference of the United Methodist Church. Watts holds a Bachelor of Arts in Theology, a Master of Divinity degree, a Doctor of Ministry degree, and a Doctor of Philosophy degree which he received from the Graduate Theological Foundation upon successfully defending his dissertation in Oxford, England, where he studied at Christ Church College, Oxford University.

www.ingramcontent.com/pod-product-compliance
Lightning Source LLC
Chambersburg PA
CBHW030842090426
42737CB00009B/1067